THE ENCYCLOPEDIA OF
KNITTING

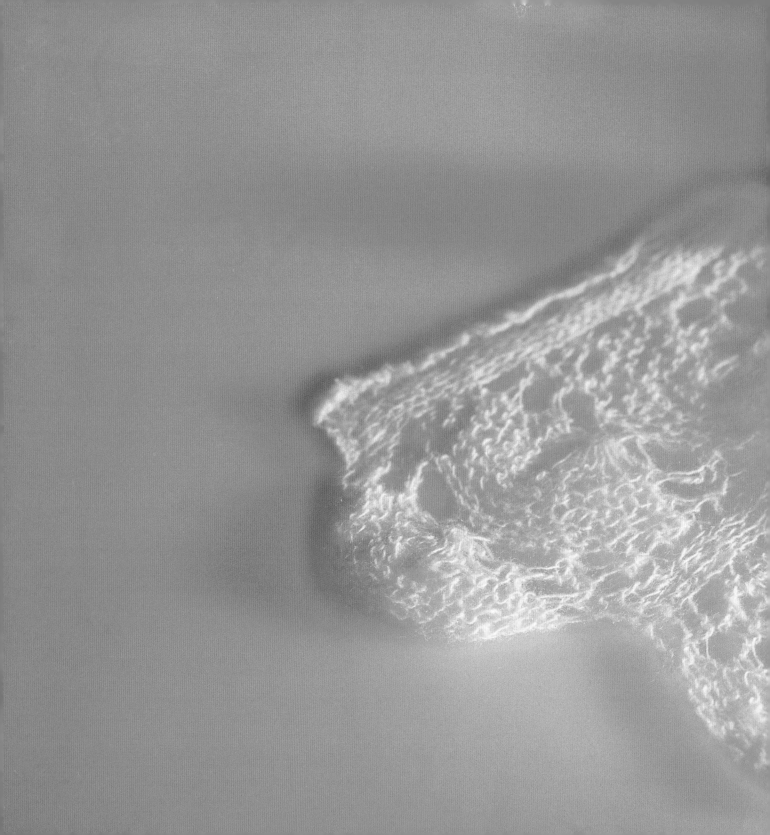

THE ENCYCLOPEDIA OF
KNITTING

by Lesley Stanfield & Melody Griffiths

APPLE

A QUARTO BOOK

Published by
Apple Press
The Old Brewery
6 Blundell Street
London N7 9BH

Copyright © 2000 Quarto Inc.

ISBN 1-84092-290-7

QUAR.EKT

Conceived, designed, and produced by
Quarto Publishing plc
The Old Brewery
6 Blundell Street
London N7 9BH

Senior project editor   Nicolette Linton
Senior Art editor   Elizabeth Healey
Designers   Caroline Grimshaw, Jenny Dooge
Text editors   Eleanor Van Zandt, Claire Waite
Pattern checker   Sue Horan
Illustrators   Ch'en Ling, Jenny Dooge
Picture researcher   Laurent Boubounelle
Indexer   Pamela Ellis

Art director   Moira Clinch
Publisher   Piers Spence

Manufactured by Regent Publishing Services Ltd, Hong Kong
Printed by Leefung-Asco Printers Ltd, China

Contents

Introduction   6

THE ESSENTIALS

Materials   10
Basic skills   14
Essential know-how   22
Additional know-how   32

THE STITCH COLLECTION

Knit and purl   44
Ribs   54
Cables   64
Twists   74
Lace   84
Bobbles and leaves   94
Stranded color knitting   104
Intarsia color knitting   114
Special effects   124

DESIGN AND INSPIRATION

How to design   136
Gallery   146

Key to chart symbols and abbreviations   156
Glossary and index   158
Credits   160

▼ Ideas for motifs can be found everywhere – from old prints to antique textiles.

Introduction

Knitting is the art of constructing a flexible fabric from a notionally continuous thread. The surface of the fabric can be smooth or textured, and the knitted pieces can be flat or tubular, straight or shaped, in infinite variety. All you need to know to get started is how to hold the yarn and needles, how to cast on and off, and the two basic stitches – knit and purl. When you're familiar with shapings and have tried out more techniques, there's the Stitch Collection to explore with its mixture of old and new stitch patterns. Then browse through Design and Inspiration to gain the confidence to create knitting that's all your own work.

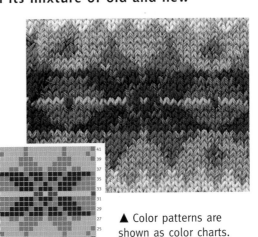

▲ These richly patterned Peruvian hats are recent examples of an old tradition.

▲ Symbols are used to explain textured stitch patterns.

▲ Color patterns are shown as color charts.

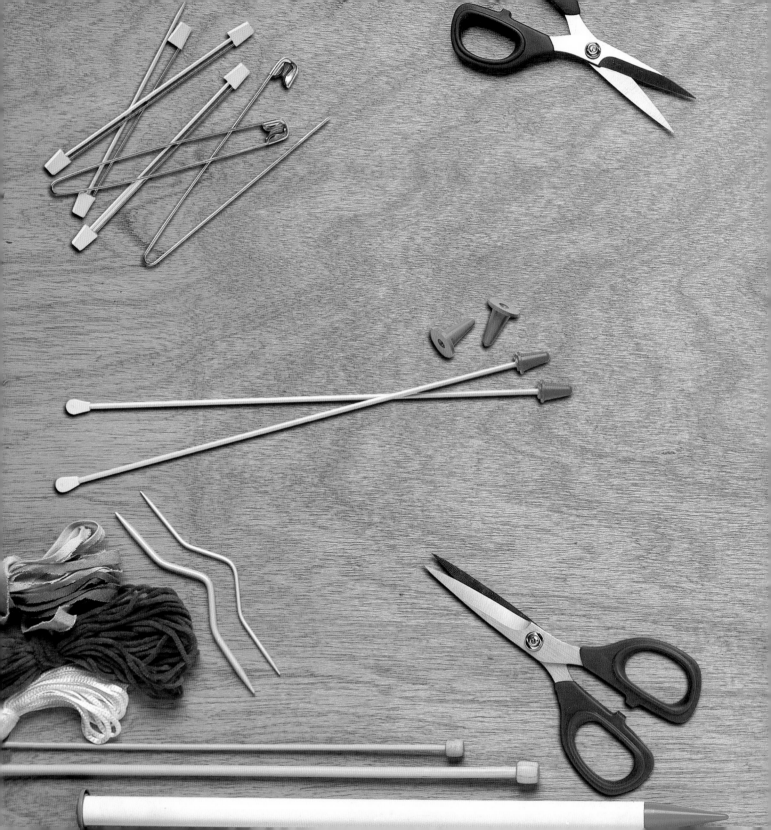

THE
ESSENTIALS

MATERIALS

You don't need complicated or expensive equipment to learn to knit – just knitting needles and yarn. As you progress in the craft, you can collect more equipment and enjoy using all kinds of yarn.

To experiment with different yarns and gauges, you'll need knitting needles in different sizes, a cable needle for working cable-stitch patterns, and double-pointed needles, or a circular needle if you want to try knitting in the round.

When you're ready to knit a garment, you'll need a tape measure or ruler, stitch holders, scissors, a tapestry or wool needle, and maybe a few other items of equipment.

Feeling the yarn as it slips through your fingers is one of the pleasures of knitting. Add to that enjoyment by exploring a whole range of yarns, from fine and smooth to bulky and textured, in synthetic blends and natural fibers.

ESSENTIAL EQUIPMENT

Knitting needles are an investment because you'll use them time and time again. Look after your needles carefully and they'll last for years, but when the points are damaged or the needles are bent, it's time to throw them out and buy new ones.

◄ Pairs of needles are made in a variety of lengths ranging from around 10in (25cm) to 16in (40cm). Most knitting needles are aluminum, usually with a pearl-gray finish, though some are nickel plated. Larger-size needles are made of plastic to reduce their weight. Bamboo needles are a flexible alternative.

◄ Double-pointed needles are sold in sets of four or five, and in several lengths. They were traditionally made of steel, but aluminum needles are more usual now, with bamboo and plastic in some sizes.

► Circular needles are simply two short needle ends joined by a flexible nylon or plastic cord. The length of a circular needle is measured from needle tip to needle tip. Most sizes are in lengths of 16in (40cm) to 47in (120cm).

► This knitting needle gauge has metric sizes on the one side, American and imperial sizes on the other.

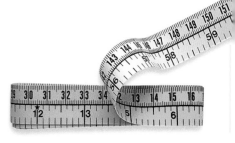

► The most useful tape measures have both inches and centimeters on the same side, so that you can compare measurements.

▶ Choose scissors that are not too small and not too large but very sharp.

▶ You'll need blunt-pointed needles – either tapestry needles or wool needles in different sizes for different weights of yarn.

▶ A crochet hook rescues dropped stitches and can be used to cast off. A row counter helps keep your place. Little point protectors stop the stitches from jumping off the needle if you have to leave your knitting in the middle of a row.

OTHER USEFUL ITEMS

You'll find some of these knitter's notions helpful when trying out different knitting techniques.

▲ Bobbins can keep yarns from tangling when working intarsia designs. A knitter's thimble can be used for color knitting.

◀ Some cable needles have a kink or crank to help keep the stitches on the needle.

FINALLY, FOR FUN

Though not strictly necessary, pompon rings and a knitting bobbin are great for getting children interested in handling yarn; They also make short work of creating decorative extras.

YARNS

We're lucky to have so many well-spun, reliable yarns to choose from. Both natural and synthetic fibers are spun into a huge variety of smooth and textured yarns, so you're bound to find something you'll enjoy knitting with.

Yarn is presented either as a ready-wound ball or a wind-it-yourself hank. The fiber content and construction determine how much yarn you'll get for the weight, so two balls that weigh the same may be very different sizes or contain very different lengths of yarn. Whatever you choose, buy the best you can afford, and your knitting will last.

SILK, LINEN AND ALPACA.

SMOOTH YARNS

Sometimes called classic yarns, these smooth yarns in wool, cotton, or mixed fibers are the knitter's reliable friends. However fine or thick these yarns are, they will always show up stitch patterns beautifully.

BRUSHED MOHAIR YARNS.

Smooth yarn

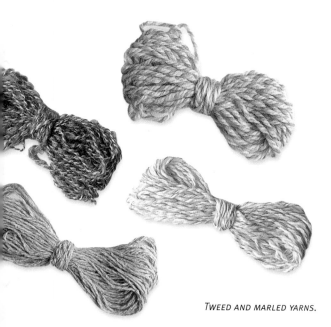

TWEED AND MARLED YARNS.

NOVELTY YARNS

Also called fashion yarns, these change from season to season. Chenille's velvety texture is a perennial favorite. One year tweedy bouclés fill the stores, next time you look everything's metallic. Shiny ribbons or richly textured blends – try them all.

TEXTURED YARNS

Fibers such as alpaca, silk, and linen make yarns that look smooth in the ball but have a distinct character when knitted. Mohair and angora can be used alone or mixed with other fibers for a soft and fluffy surface. Flecked and marled yarns give a tweedy effect, while roving yarns are single-ply and loosely twisted, giving a hand-spun look.

Textured yarn

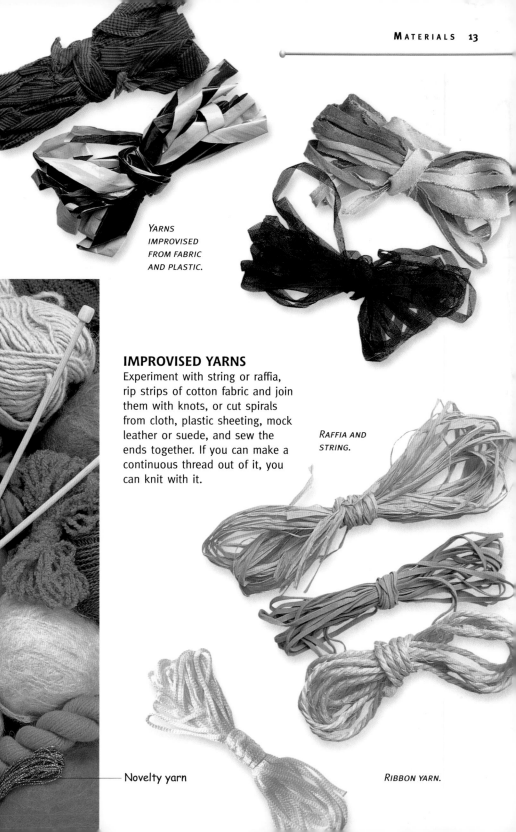

YARNS IMPROVISED FROM FABRIC AND PLASTIC.

IMPROVISED YARNS

Experiment with string or raffia, rip strips of cotton fabric and join them with knots, or cut spirals from cloth, plastic sheeting, mock leather or suede, and sew the ends together. If you can make a continuous thread out of it, you can knit with it.

RAFFIA AND STRING.

Novelty yarn

RIBBON YARN.

BASIC SKILLS: GETTING STARTED

Knitting is a two-handed craft where stitches are worked off the left needle and on to the right. To get started, sit comfortably and relax! Knitting requires hand and eye co-ordination, which is hard to achieve if you're tense.

Controlling the yarn and needles

There are many ways to hold and control the yarn and needles, but there is no one right method. Experiment until you find one that suits you.

Start by running the yarn through your fingers – see how the holds shown right all have the yarn over the forefinger ready to make a stitch. Next, pick up the needles, take one in each hand and try out the holds shown far right. Practice the steps on the following pages and soon you'll be knitting smoothly and rhythmically.

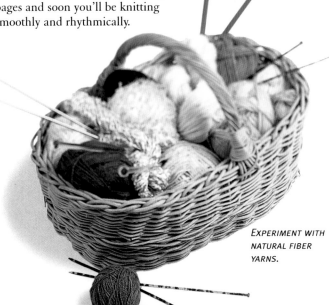

EXPERIMENT WITH NATURAL FIBER YARNS.

Holding the yarn

To feed the yarn on to the needle evenly, run it through and around your fingers, leaving the fingertips free to manipulate the needles and control the yarn.

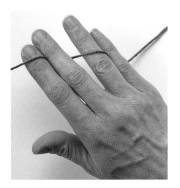 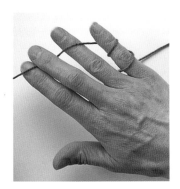

The simplest method (above left) is to slip the yarn over and under the fingers of the right hand. Wrapping the yarn around the little finger tensions it more firmly (above right).

 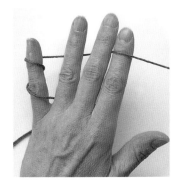

If you want to hold the yarn in your left hand, try taking it over, under and around the fingers (above left). Alternatively, wrap the yarn around the little finger, then under and over the other fingers (above right).

Holding the needles

Some knitters hold the right needle like a pen. Others hold it overhand like a knife. With the free-needle, or pen hold, the needles used are as short as is practical, and the weight of the knitting on the right needle is supported by the hand and wrist. With the fixed-needle, or knife hold, long needles are used, and the right needle is tucked under the arm for support.

If you're a beginner

Try these steps, and those on the following pages, using medium-size needles and a smooth, medium-weight pure wool yarn.

▲ FIXED NEEDLE
With your right hand, pick up a needle, hold it overhand like a knife, and tuck the end of the needle under your arm. Take the other needle in your left hand, holding it lightly over the top. Practice moving the left needle against the right. When you start knitting, you'll find you can let go of the right needle each time you make a stitch.

▲ FREE NEEDLE
With your right hand, pick up a needle, and hold it like a pen. Take the other needle in your left hand, holding it lightly with your hand over the top. Try moving the needles forward and back with your fingertips, keeping your elbows relaxed at your sides. When you cast on and start knitting, don't drop the right needle to manipulate the yarn, but support it in the crook of your thumb, and use your forefinger to control the yarn.

▲ LEFT HAND
With your right hand, pick up a needle, and hold it like a pen. With your left hand, pick up the other needle. When knitting, hold the yarn taut with the left hand while hooking or catching it with the point of the right-hand needle.

CASTING ON

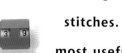

The first step in beginning any piece of knitting is to cast on some stitches. Here are three of the most useful ways to cast on.

The two-needle cable cast-on makes a strong edge with a rope-like twist, but it's not very elastic. The thumb cast-on uses just one needle and is very versatile. It's very compatible with ribs due to its elasticity. Used with garter stitch, it's indistinguishable from the rest of the knitting as it is, in effect, a knit row. The loop cast-on also uses one needle; it's simple and useful for buttonholes.

Slip knot

Putting a slip knot on the needle makes your first stitch. You can coil the yarn around your fingers or lay it flat.

1 Coil the yarn into a loop, bring forward the strand underneath, and insert the needle as shown.

2 Pull one end to tighten the knot, then gently pull the other end of the yarn to close the knot up to the needle. You're ready to cast on.

KNITTING ACCESSORIES LIKE THIS ANTIQUE YARN HOLDER CAN STILL BE USED TODAY.

Cable cast-on

This cast-on is made by knitting a stitch, then transfering it from the right to the left needle.

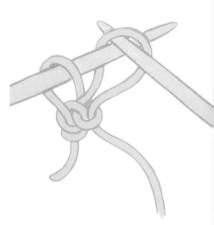

1 Leaving a short end, make a slip knot on one needle. Holding this needle in the left hand, insert the other needle into the front of the slip stitch. Take the yarn around the right needle, and pull through a stitch, then transfer it to the left needle.

2 From now on, insert the right needle between the stitches each time. Transfer each new stitch to the left needle as before.

TIP

A less robust cast-on is made if you take the needle into the stitch, instead of between stitches. This edge is useful for hems.

Loop cast-on

Tension the yarn carefully for this very basic cast-on.

Thumb cast-on

Using this method, you simply knit each stitch off your thumb.

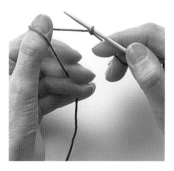

1 Measure off about three times the length of the edge to be cast on and make a slip knot on the needle. Hold the needle and yarn from the ball in your right hand.

2 Tensioning the other end in your left hand, make a loop around your thumb, and insert the right needle in the loop.

3 Take the yarn around the needle. Then draw a loop through to make a stitch. Gently pull the end to close the stitch up to the needle. Repeat until the required number of stitches, including the slip stitch, have been cast on.

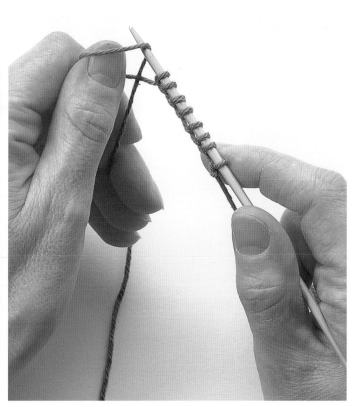

▲ Leaving a short end, make a slip knot on the needle. Tension the yarn in your left hand, and make a loop around your thumb. Insert the needle in the loop, slip your thumb out, and gently pull the yarn to make a stitch on the needle.

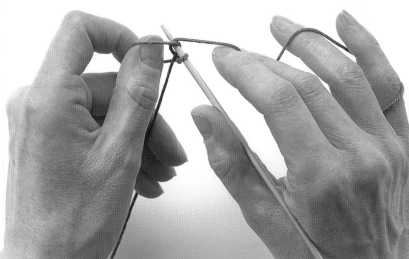

KNIT AND PURL

THE KNIT STITCH

When you've mastered the thumb cast-on, you'll find the knit stitch – the most basic of stitches – very familiar.

Garter Stitch

If you knit every stitch of every row, the result is garter stitch. Although it's very simple, this reversible fabric can be very versatile. Knitted loosely, it's soft and springy. Worked firmly, the fabric lies flat, which makes it useful for bands and borders. Garter stitch makes an elastic fabric in which the stitches are stretched widthwise, while the rows draw up to give an almost square gauge.

Making a knit stitch

Choose to hold the yarn and needles in whichever way you feel most comfortable.

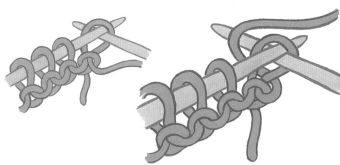

1 Insert the right needle into the first stitch on the left needle. Make sure it goes from left to right into the front of the stitch.

2 Taking the yarn behind, bring it up and around the right needle.

3 Using the tip of the right needle, draw a loop of yarn through the stitch.

4 Slip the stitch off the left needle. There is now a new stitch on the right needle.

Knitting a row

Continue making stitches on the right needle until all stitches have been worked off the left needle, then hold the needle with the stitches in the left hand for the next row. You'll soon find that the movements flow into each other as you pick up more speed.

CREATE A SIMPLE SCARF WITH BASIC STOCKINETTE STITCH.

THE PURL STITCH

To progress to stockinette and more stitch patterns, you'll need to know how to purl. Purling isn't difficult – just think of it as the opposite of a knit stitch.

Making a purl stitch

Hold the yarn and needles in the same way as for making a knit stitch.

1 Insert the right needle into the first stitch on the left needle. Make sure it goes into the stitch from right to left.

2 Taking the yarn to the front, loop it around the right needle.

3 Lower the tip of the right needle, taking it away from you to draw a loop of yarn through the stitch.

4 Slip the stitch off the left needle. There is now a new stitch on the right needle.

Stockinette stitch

The best known combination of knit and purl is called stockinette stitch. It's very simple, just knit one row and purl one row alternately.

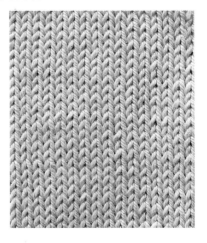

Reverse stockinette stitch

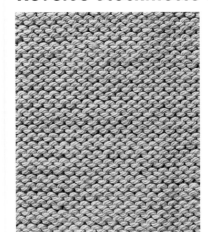

The right side of stockinette is smooth and the other side is ridged. If you use the ridged side as the right side of the piece, it is called reverse stockinette.

TIP

To count rows in stockinette stitch, count the ridges on the reverse. For garter stitch, count each ridge as two rows.

CASTING OFF

Casting off – also called binding off – links stitches to make a neat edge that won't unravel.

Although there's one basic method of casting off, there are simple variations that can be useful. Chain cast-off is the easiest and most used. The decrease cast-off is less well known, but gives a very smooth finish. Casting off with a crochet hook makes it easy to cope with slippery yarns or tight stitches.

These diagrams show casting off on the right side of stockinette, however you can cast off on a wrong-side row or in knit and purl, depending on the stitch pattern.

IT CAN BE MORE DIFFICULT TO DETECT A DROPPED STITCH WHEN USING FLUFFY WOOLS LIKE MOHAIR.

Chain cast-off

Lifting one stitch over the next makes a chain along the top of the knitting on the side the cast-off is worked.

1 Start by knitting the first two stitches. Use the point of the left needle to lift the first of these stitches over the second stitch and off the needle.

2 Knit the next stitch so that there are two stitches on the right needle, then lift the first over the second. Repeat until there is one stitch left. Break the yarn, draw it through the stitch, and pull it tight.

TIP

If your chain cast-off is too tight, especially at a neck edge, cast off with a needle one or more sizes larger.

Decrease cast-off

This cast-off doesn't make a chain, so it's useful for an edge that is going to be sewn down.

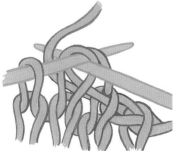

1 Knit the first two stitches together, then slip the stitch just made on to the left needle.

2 Knit together the first two stitches on the left needle, the one already worked and the next one. Slip the stitch just made on to the left needle, as before. Repeat until one stitch is left. Break the yarn, draw it through the stitch, and pull it tight.

Crochet cast-off

This cast-off can be as tight or as loose as necessary, according to the tensioning of the crochet chain.

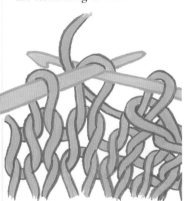

Hold the yarn in your left hand. Slip the first stitch on to the hook. Insert the hook into the next stitch, catch the yarn, and pull it through both stitches. Repeat to the last stitch, break the yarn, and pull it through.

PICKING UP A DROPPED STITCH

Don't panic if you drop a stitch. Here's how to get it back on the needle.

Stop the stitch as soon as you can. Use the needles or a crochet hook to pull the unraveled strands through to make the stitches.

1 If the stitch has dropped one or two rows, lift the strand on to the needle behind the dropped stitch. Use the left needle to take the stitch over the strand, and lift the new stitch back on to the left needle, making sure it faces the correct way.

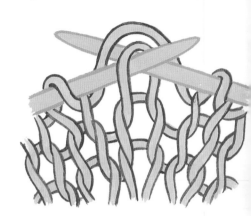

2 If the stitch has dropped a long way, insert the hook through the dropped stitch from the front, then catch the strand, and pull it through to make a new stitch. Put the last stitch on the left needle. Each strand of the ladder is a row, so make sure you catch all of them.

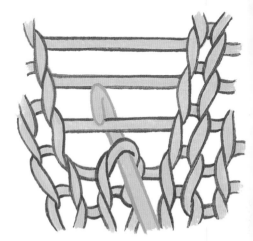

ESSENTIAL KNOW-HOW: SHAPINGS

Now you know the basics, you'll want to make something to wear. Here's how to shape your knitting, follow instructions, and sew up your work beautifully.

When shaping your knitting, increases make the fabric wider and decreases make it narrower. Increases and decreases can also be used to create stitch patterns.

   In this section, you'll also learn the simple technique of picking up stitches – the best way to start a neckband and all kinds of edgings. Understanding the instructions for the design you've chosen is easy if you take it one step at a time. Charts are a wonderfully clear explanation of stitch patterns, and are simple to use once you know how. And you'll discover that the secret of a beautiful garment is knitting to the correct gauge and knowing the best way to sew up for a perfect finish.

☞

**Decreases page 24
Picking up Stitches page 25
Reading Patterns and Charts
pages 26 – 27**

SIMPLE SHAPINGS

When knitting, you can shape at the same time as creating the fabric.

One-stitch increases and decreases are used to shape sleeves, armholes and necks. They can be both practical and decorative. Fully fashioned shapings are made several stitches in from the edges, so that the increases and decreases become a feature of the design. Shapings can also be used across a row, for example, stitches may be increased or decreased at the top of a rib.

FULLY FASHIONED SHAPING
These bar increases are made to look as though they are two stitches in from the edge.

BUYING YARN ON CONES CAN BE VERY ECONOMICAL.

INCREASES

Here are two of the most basic methods of increasing a stitch – bar increase and lifted strand increase.

Bar increase on a knit row

Knitting into the front and the back of a stitch is the most common increase. It's a neat, firm increase which makes a little bar on the right side of the work at the base of the new stitch. This makes it easy to count rows between shapings.

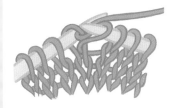 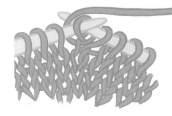

1 Knit into the front of the stitch, and pull the loop through, but leave the stitch on the left needle.

2 Knit into the back of the stitch on the left needle.

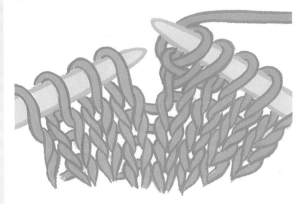

3 Slip the stitch off the left needle making two stitches on the right needle. Note that the bar of the new stitch lies on the left.

To increase on a purl row

Either purl into the front and back of the stitch, or purl into a lifted strand.

Lifted strand increase on a knit row

Making a stitch from the strand between the stitches is a very neat way to increase. Because it's almost invisible it's useful for shaping in color knitting.

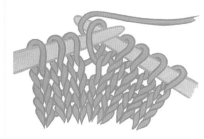

1 Pick up the strand between the stitches with the left needle. Make sure the strand lies on the needle in the same direction as the other stitches, then knit into the back of it.

BALANCING LIFTED-STRAND INCREASES
If you're shaping at the sides of a garment, work lifted-strand increases one or more stitches in from each edge – allowing the same number of stitches before and after the increase. If you're shaping a dart, leave one or more stitches between increases.

Balancing increases

If you work a bar increase into the first stitch in a row, the increase will appear one stitch in, so the edge will be smooth. Make the increase at the end of the row in the last stitch but one, and the bar will also sit one stitch in from the edge. Lifted-strand increases can be made the same number of stitches in from each edge. Perfectionists will turn the strand in the opposite direction at each end of a row.

SHAPINGS

DECREASES

Decreases – like increases – have two basic functions. They can be used to reduce the number of stitches in a row, as in armholes and necklines or, combined with increases, they can create stitch patterns.

Right-slanting decreases

Knitting two stitches together makes a smooth shaping with the second stitch lying on top of the first.

1 Insert the right needle through the front of the first two stitches on the left needle, then take the yarn around the needle.

2 Draw the loop through and drop the two stitches off the left needle.

☞
**Understanding Gauge
pages 28 – 29
Making Up pages 30 – 31
Design and Inspiration
pages 134 – 145**

Left-slanting decrease

Slipping a stitch, knitting a stitch, then lifting the slipped stitch over, makes a shaping with the first stitch lying on top of the second.

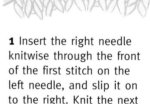

1 Insert the right needle knitwise through the front of the first stitch on the left needle, and slip it on to the right. Knit the next stitch.

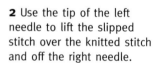

2 Use the tip of the left needle to lift the slipped stitch over the knitted stitch and off the right needle.

Balancing decreases

Work the decreases in pairs, using complementary methods. For a smooth line of shapings, work a decrease slanting left near the beginning of the row, and a decrease slanting right near the end. For a feathered effect, reverse the decreases.

NORMAL DECREASE

FEATHERED DECREASE

PICKING UP STITCHES

This technique is vital for a well-finished garment as it eliminates bulky seams.

Picking up stitches is simply knitting up new stitches along an edge ready to work a band or border in another direction.

HOW TO PICK UP A STITCH

Hold the knitting with the right side toward you, insert the needle under an edge stitch, take the yarn around and pull a loop through to make a stitch. When you have picked up enough stitches, remember the next row will be a wrong-side row.

PICKING UP ALONG A STRAIGHT EDGE

The secret of a satisfactory picked-up edge is to pick up the right number of stitches. When picking up from row-ends, don't work into every row end or your band will flare. Skip row ends at regular intervals so that your band will lie flat. To pick up along a cast-on or cast-off edge, work into every stitch.

PICKING UP ALONG A SHAPED EDGE

Don't skip stitches along the shaped edges of a neckline, but work into every decrease and row end. When picking up from a stitch pattern, space the number of stitches as necessary to fit in with the pattern.

 TIP

To pick up a given number of stitches along an edge, fold it in half, mark the halfway point, then fold each half and mark the quarters. Divide the number of stitches by four, and pick up this number of stitches evenly from each marked quarter.

READING PATTERNS AND CHARTS

Reading a knitting pattern may be unfamiliar at first, but as soon as you've cracked the code, you'll be able to follow instructions with confidence.

You've found your dream design, but how can you be sure your sweater will fit? What should you buy? What do abbreviations mean, and how do you read a chart?

OLD KNITTING PATTERNS CAN BE FASCINATING.

What are the measurements?

The sizes will be set out in sequence, as a grid or with larger sizes in brackets. Because fit varies so much from one design to another, first compare the actual bust or chest measurement with your body measurement, then check the length and sleeves. Some garments are designed to fit closely, while others are very loose – choose the fit you want.

What do you need to buy?

It's important to buy the yarn specified. Another yarn, however similar, may not behave in the same way and you might need a different amount. Make sure you buy enough yarn – and check that you have everything else listed, such as a cable needle.

Checking your gauge

Gauge is given as the number of stitches and rows, usually to 4in (10cm), over the stitch pattern on the recommended size needles. The needle size should be treated as a guide only – you may need to use a different size to knit to the gauge given in the instructions. See page 28 for more about gauge.

Understanding abbreviations

Once you're familiar with abbreviations, you'll find it quicker and easier to find your way around the instructions. Some abbreviations are simply the first letter of the word, for example "k" for "knit". Others use the first few letters, such as "rep" for "repeat". Sometimes the first letters of several words are run together, for example "skpo" for "slip one, knit one, pass the slipped stitch over". Not all knitting instructions use the same abbreviations. For instance, "k1b" may mean "knit in the back of the stitch", or as in this book "knit in the row below". So always read the abbreviations each time you follow a new set of instructions.

Understanding repeats

Knitting is full of repetitition. Stitch patterns repeat horizontally across a row and vertically over several rows. These multiples can either be shown on a chart or explained in words. Round or square brackets can be used to enclose instructions which are to be repeated. For example "[k2, p2] 3 times", is a concise way to write "k2, p2, k2, p2, k2, p2".

Asterisks are also used as markers to indicate a repeat. For example, "rep from * to **" means "repeat the instructions contained between the asterisks as many times as given".

When two parts of a garment share the same instructions, a group of asterisks is used to indicate the sections that are the same and where they differ.

Reading charts

Charts are a visual explanation of stitches and rows. They are a very efficient way to check your place in a pattern repeat or to compare one repeat with another. Each square usually represents one stitch. The key will explain the colors or symbols.

Charts are always numbered from the bottom to the top because this is the direction of the knitting. The first row may be either a right or a wrong side row. Right side rows are read from right to left and wrong side rows are read from left to right. The multiple of the pattern repeat is sometimes shown underneath the chart, while shaded areas or dotted lines indicate extra or end stitches.

UNDERSTANDING CHARTS

Color knitting charts

Most color knitting is in stockinette, so every right side row is knit and every wrong side row is purl, with the squares on the chart showing the color to be used. The chart may be printed in color or may use a symbol for each color. If any textured stitches are used, they will be shown as symbols and explained in the key.

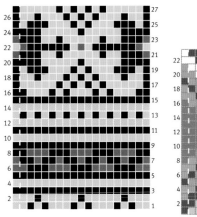 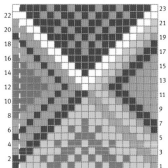

Reading charts

Every stitch and every row is shown as on the right side of the knitting. A blank square represents knit on a right side row and purl on a wrong side row – making stockinette. A dot represents purl on a right side row and knit on a wrong side row – making reverse stockinette.

Some symbols represent more than one stitch, such as a decrease. Where the stitch count varies within a stitch pattern, solid areas compensate for the missing stitches.

Not all methods of charting use the same symbols, so always check the key.

TIP

Enlarging a chart by photocopying can make it easier to follow. Make several copies and glue or tape them together. If it helps, draw any shapings on the photocopy.

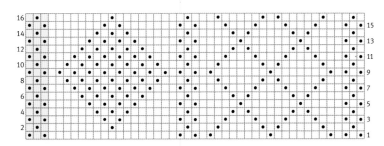

UNDERSTANDING GAUGE

The gauge of a piece of knitting is the number of stitches and rows counted over a given measurement. Gauge is controlled by the type of yarn, the size of the needles, and the stitch pattern. It is crucial to a successful result.

A designer will establish the number of stitches and rows needed to obtain a given measurement in the chosen yarn – usually 4 inches or 10 centimeters – and stitch pattern, and use that information when calculating the size and shape of a garment. So it is vital for the knitter following the instructions to work to the same gauge, otherwise the garment simply won't measure the same.

Knitting patterns emphasize that the knitter must use the correct yarn, so you might think that this applies to the needle size too. But the needle size is given as a guide only, it doesn't matter what size you use as long as you get the correct gauge.

So always knit up a swatch and check your gauge before you start on the real thing. It's the only way to save wasting time and effort, creating a knit that doesn't fit.

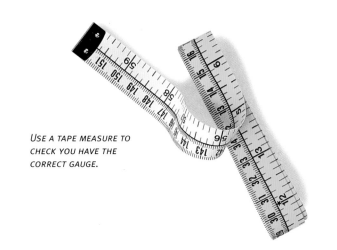

USE A TAPE MEASURE TO CHECK YOU HAVE THE CORRECT GAUGE.

HOW TO MEASURE GAUGE

Knit a swatch with the size needles given in the instructions. Always add a few extra stitches and work a few more rows because the edge stitches will be distorted. Check the making up instructions and, if necessary, press your swatch. Measure the gauge on a flat surface.

MEASURING STITCHES

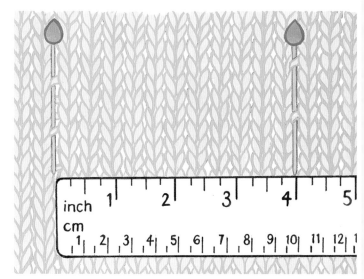

1 Count and mark the stitches with pins, then measure between the pins. If the measurement is correct, you'll know that your finished garment will be the right width. If your marked stitches measure less, you're knitting too tightly and the garment will be too narrow. Knit another swatch using larger needles, and measure again. If the marked stitches measure more than they should, you're knitting loosely and the garment will be too wide. Knit another swatch on smaller needles, and measure again.

TIP

The ball band often gives the manufacturer's recommended stockinette gauge, but you should always check your gauge in the stitch pattern as well.

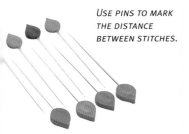

HOW NEEDLE SIZE AFFECTS GAUGE
See how the same yarn, the same number of stitches, and the same number of rows worked by the same knitter give different-size swatches depending on the size of the needles.

MEASURING STITCHES

SMALL NEEDLES

LARGE NEEDLES

MEDIUM NEEDLES

2 Mark the number of rows and check the measurement. If it's correct go ahead and start knitting. If the marked rows measure less your knitting is tight, and the garment will be too short. Try using larger needles for your next swatch. If the marked rows measure more, your knitting is loose, and the garment will be too long. Try knitting another swatch using smaller needles.

TIP *When joining in new yarn, start a new ball of yarn at the beginning of a row, where the edge will be part of a seam. Make a neat bundle with the tail end of yarn left from the old ball. To join the new yarn, make a single overhand knot. When sewing up, undo the knot, thread one end on to a sewing needle, and run it through a few stitches of the seam.*

MAKING UP

Assembling a knitted garment involves two processes – pressing each piece of knitting, then sewing them together.

Pressing

Pinning out and pressing your knitting before sewing up will make an enormous difference to the finished garment. Always check the ball band for yarn care, and test a sample swatch before applying heat or steam to your knitting – natural fiber yarns are usually quite robust, but man-made mixes can collapse and therefore need a cool, dry iron.

Pin each piece out to size with the right-side down on a padded board, using a tape measure to check the measurement. Then lay a dampened cotton muslin cloth on top, and gently apply the iron. Remember never to stamp the iron down or push it along the surface of the knitting.

If the yarn is delicate or if the stitch pattern is textured, pin out the pieces but do not press. Instead, dampen them with a water spray, then leave them to dry naturally.

Sewing up

Sewing up from the right side is the secret of invisible seams. This method, also known as ladder or mattress stitch, is good for joining side and sleeve seams in most stitch patterns.

◀ STOCKINETTE
The seam is almost invisible in stockinette stitch.

▲ INVISIBLE SEAM
Place both pieces of knitting flat, with right sides facing and the edges to be joined running vertically. Thread a wool needle with yarn and secure at one lower edge – the first side. Take the needle under the cast-on edge of the second side, draw the yarn through, then go under the first cast-on edge again. Tension the yarn to level the edges. Take the needle under the strand between the edge stitch and the next stitch on the first row of the second side, and draw the yarn through. Repeat for the first row of the first side. Continue joining row ends from alternate sides in this way, without splitting stitches.

◀ RIB
Ribbing needs to be planned, so that when the seam is joined, the stitches at each edge combine to make a whole rib.

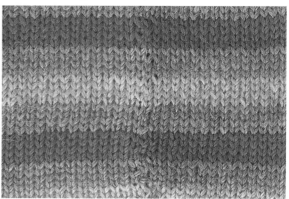

▲ STRIPES
Stripes and color patterns are easier to match when sewn together from the right side.

▶ SLIP STITCH

Catching down pocket linings or zipper facings is easy with slip stitch. With wrong sides facing, tack the pieces to be joined, matching rows. Thread a wool needle with yarn. Secure the end, then take the needle alternately under a strand on the main fabric and an edge strand. Don't let the stitches show on the right side or pull the yarn too tight.

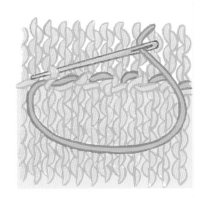

▶ BACK STITCH

Back stitch makes strong seams. Hold the pieces with right sides together. Thread a wool needle and secure the yarn at the right-hand end. Lining up rows and working one stitch in from the edge, bring the needle up through both pieces of knitting between stitches of first and second rows, then down between the first row and the cast-on edge. Come up again one or two rows on, and go down next to the previous stitch. Complete the seam in this way, taking care to work between the knitted stitches.

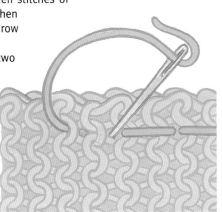

TIP

Cover your padded ironing board with a check fabric to help you line up the rows and stitches when pinning out.

Perfecting your technique

NEAT DROP SHOULDERS

If you're joining a straight cast-off sleeve top to the row ends of a back and front to make a drop shoulder, don't match stitch-for-stitch. Skip a few row ends at regular intervals to compensate for the different stitch and row gauges.

▶ POCKET LININGS

To keep pocket linings square when stitching them down, tack contrast color guidelines between the stitches on the right side each side of the pocket opening. Turn over and follow the tacked guidelines to sew the pocket linings down.

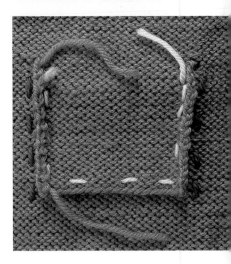

PERFECT PRESSING

Knitting can be molded into shape at the pressing stage if it's wool or cotton. Buy or make a tailor's ham – an overstuffed fabric ball – for pressing set-in sleeve heads.

ADDITIONAL KNOW-HOW

The basic skills will take you a long way in knitting, but sometimes more unusual techniques can make all the difference. Learning how and when to use these alternatives is the first step towards designing for yourself.

Interesting cast-on or cast-off edgings can transform a simple garment. Tailored effects such as hems and facings give a sophisticated look to knitting and are often the best solution when planning borders for color or intarsia knitting. Grafting is a useful emergency technique for changing the length of a piece of knitting, and can be adapted to make almost invisible seams. Turning rows are a subtle way to shape within the fabric of the knitting, while adding more increases and decreases to your knitting knowledge will help make perfect shapings and more elaborate stitch patterns.

MORE CASTING ON AND OFF

Here are two more ways to cast on and to cast off, each with their own characteristics.

CHANNEL ISLAND CAST-ON

Strongly defined knots decorate the edge of this robust cast-on. For an odd number of stitches, work as given here. For an even number of stitches, simply cast on one more stitch at the end.

◀ Leaving an end six times the length of the edge to be cast on, put a slip knot on one needle. Double this length back on itself so that the free end hangs down where it meets the needle at the slip knot. Take the doubled end in your left hand and the single strand from the ball in your right hand. Wind the doubled end twice around the thumb of your left hand. Insert the needle up and under both of the double strands of yarn on your thumb, and take the single strand around the needle to make a stitch. Pull on the ends to bring the knot up the needle. Bring the single strand forward and over the needle to make a stitch. Continue to make pairs of stitches in this way, ending with a stitch knitted from the thumb.

◀ The decorative quality of this cast-on can be seen on the lower edge of a typical Guernsey-style sweater.

KNOTTED CAST-ON

Casting on by this method makes a small knot at the base of each stitch and gives an attractive double-strength edge.

◄ Leaving an end about four times the length of the edge to be cast on, make a slip knot on one needle. Cast on one stitch by the thumb method, lift the slip knot over the stitch. Cast on two more stitches, and take the first of the two over the second for each cast-on stitch required.

PICOT CAST-OFF

Instead of a plain cast-off, try this very pretty finish. The picots can be made on every stitch, in which case the edge will flute, or they can be spaced with as many chain cast-off stitches between as are needed to make the edge lie flat.

► Insert the right needle into the first stitch on the left needle, and knit a stitch but do not slip the stitch off the left needle. Slip the new stitch on to the left needle, then make a second new stitch as before. Cast off four stitches, then slip the remaining stitch back on to the left needle. Repeat along the row, making two stitches and casting off four each time.

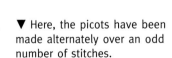

▼ Here, the picots have been made alternately over an odd number of stitches.

CAST-OFF SEAMS

Instead of joining back and front shoulder edges, by casting them off separately and sewing them together, a softer join is made if the two sets of stitches are cast off together. This can be done invisibly on the wrong side, as shown here, or made into a feature by being cast off with the wrong sides together.

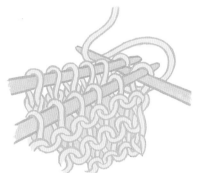

1 Do not cast off the shoulder stitches, but leave them on spare needles. Place the back and front shoulders together with right sides facing and needles pointing in the same direction. Using a third needle, knit the first stitch on the near needle together with the first stitch on the back needle.

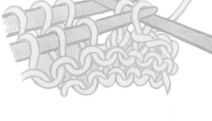

2 Knit the next pair of stitches together, and then take the first stitch on the right needle over the second, in the usual way. Continue until all the stitches have been cast off. When casting off two pieces of knitting with wrong sides together, make sure that the chain edge of the cast-off faces the same way on each shoulder.

TIP

If you want to join shaped shoulder seams in this way, don't cast off groups of stitches, but work turning rows instead. The shoulders can then be cast off together.

HEMS AND FACINGS

Instead of making edgings in rib or garter stitch, you can make hems or facings for a more substantial double-fabric finish.

These techniques owe more to dressmaking than to knitting, but they can be very successful if the right design and yarn are chosen.

MITERED CORNERS

Where a hem and a facing meet, or between an edging and a front band, a mitered corner may be the neatest solution. For this you need to increase or decrease to make a 45-degree angle. Shaping on alternate rows in garter stitch or moss stitch produces this angle almost perfectly. In stockinette, achieving the correct angle may entail shaping on a mixture of alternate rows and every row, because the stitches are wider than they are tall.

▲ Here, the garter-stitch edging and front band form a neatly mitered corner.

PLAIN HEM

A knitted hem can be turned up and slip stitched in the same way as a woven fabric hem. This can be bulky, and the folded edge may spread, so it's preferable to make a neat knitted-in hem.

▶ With smaller needles than for the main fabric, cast on fairly loosely using the loop method. Work the depth of the hem in stockinette stitch. Mark the fold with a ridge by working a row out of sequence – either three purl rows or three knit rows, the center row of the three making the ridge. Change to the needles for the main fabric and continue in stockinette stitch until the depth from the ridge matches that of the hem, ending with a purl row. To join the hem on the next row, fold the hem up behind the main fabric, then knit together the first stitch from the left needle with the first stitch from the cast-on edge. Continue in this way to the end of the row.

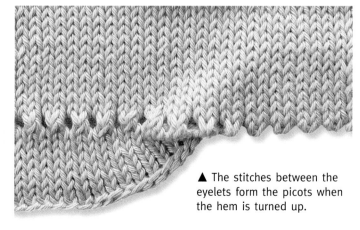

PICOT HEM

A very attractive way to mark the fold of a hem is to work a row of eyelets, which, when the hem is turned up, makes a row of well-defined picots. Work to the depth of the hem, ending with a wrong-side row. If the work contains an odd number of stitches, work the next row: k1, *yo, k2tog; rep from * to end. Over an even number of stitches, begin the row k2.

▲ The stitches between the eyelets form the picots when the hem is turned up.

FACINGS

Unlike ribbon or fabric, a knitted stockinette facing will be flexible and a perfect color match. For the front edges of a jacket or cardigan, the facing is best worked in one with the main part. To ensure that the facing folds on the same stitch along its length, slip this stitch on every right-side row.

▲ The slipped stitch forms a natural fold line for a facing.

FASTENINGS

If you're knitting a garment that requires some form of fastening, here's how to make it as neat as possible.

BUTTONHOLES

Buttonholes are best kept simple. Knitted fabric does not lend itself to the detailed finishing used on woven fabric, so try to make buttonholes neat enough to make buttonhole stitching afterward unnecessary, as this reduces size and flexibility and can be clumsy.

EYELET BUTTONHOLES

A single or double eyelet is often sufficient for a small buttonhole. A single eyelet is made with a yarn-over and single decrease; a double eyelet is made with a double yarn-over and a balanced decrease on either side.

HORIZONTAL BUTTONHOLES

The simplest method is to cast off stitches on one row with a chain cast-off, and cast on the same number above them on the next row with a loop cast-on. To prevent a hole before the first stitch of the cast-on group, work into the front and back of the last stitch before the buttonhole, and cast on one stitch less.

◄ Two buttonholes, one in the front and one in the facing, come together when the facing is turned in along the line of slip stitches.

VERTICAL BUTTONHOLES

Knit along the row to the place where the buttonhole will be, turn, then work the required number of rows. Break the yarn, rejoin it where the knitting turned, and work the same number of rows on this side. Finally, work on all stitches to close the buttonhole at the top. Use the two ends of yarn left to reinforce the top and base of the buttonhole.

BUTTONS

Choose your buttons first and make the buttonholes to fit. Faced front edges or a bulky yarn may require the button to have a shank.

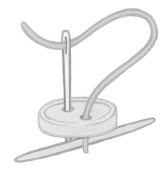

▲ To make the shank, sew on the button over a spacer such as a cable needle. When the button is secure, remove the spacer, twist the yarn around the shank, then fasten off.

ZIPPERS

Zippers are slightly incompatible with knitting, but they are sometimes more appropriate than buttons. Edge the zipper opening with a few stitches of garter stitch or moss stitch. Pin and baste the zipper in place, lining up rows or stitch patterns on either side. Open the zipper to back stitch it. For a neat finish, knit narrow facings to cover the zipper tape.

GRAFTING

Duplicating a row of stitches with yarn and a wool needle makes an invisible join in knitting. Use this technique to alter the length of a garment or adapt the method to join shoulder seams.

Always use a blunt-pointed needle to avoid splitting stitches and thread it with enough yarn to work a row. Tension the sewn stitches to match the knitting. To make an alteration, snip a stitch in the center of the row, then pick up the loops of the stitches above and the stitches of the row below as you ease out the yarn.

Working on the stitches of the lower piece, undo rows to make it shorter or add more rows to make it longer. When you're ready to graft, lay the pieces to be joined close together, with the needles pointing in the same direction. It's easiest to graft in stockinette or reverse stockinette stitch, as described here, but once you understand how to imitate the stitches you can try grafting in other stitch patterns.

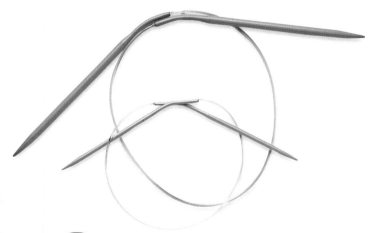

TIP

When you're undoing from the center of a row, use two circular needles: one to pick up the stitches below and the other for the loops above.

KNIT GRAFTING

Lay the pieces to be joined flat with the right sides facing so you can slip the stitches off the knitting needles as you trap them with the sewn stitches.

▲ Bring the needle up through the first stitch of the last row on the lower piece. Go down through the loop at the side edge and up in the center of the next loop on the upper piece, then go down through the first stitch of the lower piece again, and up through the next stitch. Continue until all stitches and loops are joined to make a row.

GRAFTING A SEAM

This variation on grafting is useful for joining shoulders. Because the stitches run in opposite directions, the side edges will be a half stitch out, but this can be hidden in a seam.

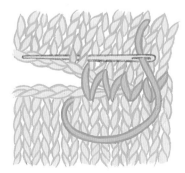

◄Thread a wool needle with yarn and bring it up through the center of the first stitch on the front. Take it under the edge stitch on the back, and down through the first stitch again. Repeat, taking in a whole stitch each time to match the front and back stitches perfectly.

PURL GRAFTING

Arrange the knitting on two needles and lay it flat. The sewn stitches will make a purl row.

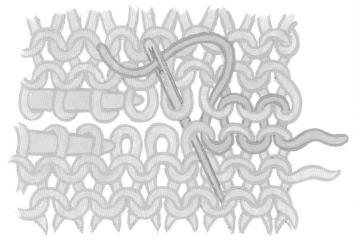

▲Bring the needle down through the first stitch on the lower piece, up through the loop at the side edge, and down in the center of the next loop on the upper piece. Then go up through the first stitch of the lower piece. Continue in this way along the row, tensioning the sewn stitches as you go.

GRAFTING GARTER STITCH

To keep the pattern correct, make sure that the lower piece of knitting ends with a ridge and the upper piece with a smooth row. To join the row, work the lower stitches as knit grafting and the upper stitches as purl grafting.

GRAFTING RIBS

Follow the pattern of the stitches, alternating knit and purl grafting. Wide ribs are easier to join than single rib.

TURNING ROWS

Short rows, made by turning and leaving stitches unworked, can be used to shape knitting.

For a steep slant, leave one or two stitches; for a gentler slope, leave more stitches unworked. For a symmetrical shaping, leave stitches unworked at both ends. For a smooth transition between rows, anchor the yarn before turning and working back.

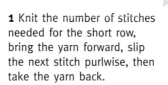

1 Knit the number of stitches needed for the short row, bring the yarn forward, slip the next stitch purlwise, then take the yarn back.

2 Return the slipped stitch to the left needle ready to turn and work the next short row.

▼ This swatch shows the use of turning rows to make a sloping edge. The stripes help you to see clearly where the yarn is taken around the slipped stitches. The same technique can be used when turning on a purl row.

MORE USEFUL DECREASES

Working three stitches together keeps rib and other stitch patterns correct when decreasing, and can be used decoratively and structurally for lace and solid-stitch patterns.

Choosing the right decrease for the stitch pattern is vital for shaping garments successfully. The single decreases shown on page 24 reduce the width of the knitting one stitch at a time, but sometimes it's necessary to take more stitches together.

A double decrease takes in the knitting more rapidly. In knit one, purl one rib, it can be placed so that the pattern is not interrupted on the next row. And in many stitch patterns, double decreases are used with double increases to create beautiful lacy effects.

All these methods of decreasing can be adapted to make multiple decreases by taking more stitches together. As with all decreases, it's very important to be aware of the position of the stitch that lies on top. Always pair a left-slanting and a right-slanting decrease when shaping a garment or working a stitch pattern. The dominant center stitch of the balanced double decrease makes a design feature of shaped darts and gives a clean line to lace patterns.

TIP

Purling several stitches together is easier than knitting them together, so try to finish off large bobbles with a purl stitch.

Right-slanting decreases

The easiest way to decrease two stitches is simply to knit three stitches together. With this decrease, the stitch furthest to the left will lie on top, giving a decrease that slants to the right. To give the same right-slanting decrease when working on the wrong side, you'll need to purl the stitches together.

KNIT THREE TOGETHER

Count the number of stitches to work into on the left needle. Insert the right needle tip into the front of the third stitch, then through the fronts of the other two stitches, take the yarn around the needle in the usual way, draw the new stitch through all three stitches and drop them off the left needle together.

PURL THREE TOGETHER

Insert the right needle into the fronts of stitches, take the yarn around the needle, and draw the new stitch through in the usual way, dropping the stitches off the left needle together.

Left-slanting decreases

For a double decrease that slants to the left, worked on a right-side row, you'll need to take the first stitch over a single decrease. For a similar-looking decrease worked on a wrong-side row, purl three together through the back of the loops.

SLIP ONE
KNIT TWO TOGETHER, PASS THE SLIPPED STITCH OVER

Slip the first stitch knitwise, knit the next two stitches together, then lift the first stitch over as shown. The first stitch lies on top, so the decrease slants to the left.

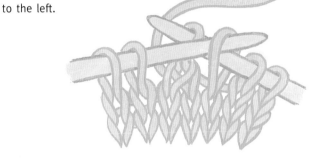

▼ To balance decreases at each side of the fabric, as shown in this swatch, work rib 5, knit three together at the beginning of the row, and at the end of the row slip one, knit two together, pass the slipped stitch over, rib 5. Because the decreases reduce three stitches to one each time, the rib pattern is correct on the following rows.

Balanced double decrease

Working a decrease that takes one stitch from each side and leaves the center stitch on top has lots of potential for shaping and for working beautiful stitch patterns.

1 Insert the right needle into the second and first stitches as if to knit two together, and slip these stitches onto the right needle.

2 Knit the next stitch, then lift the two slipped stitches over the middle stitch of the decrease lies on top.

◀ In this swatch, the ribs travel to the center and the decreased stitches are neatly hidden under the center stitch. The rib remains correct for the following rows.

MORE USEFUL INCREASES

The basic increases shown on page 23 all make one stitch. Here are two neat ways to increase two stitches.

Multiple increases are useful for lace stitches and for keeping stitch patterns – such as ribs – correct while shaping.

▲Shaping in single rib looks very decorative when double lifted increases are used. To keep the rib correct, knit into the lifted stitches to make knit stitches, and purl into the lifted stitches to make purl stitches.

WORKING TWICE INTO A YARN-OVER

If your instructions tell you to make two stitches from a double yarn-over on the previous row, try this neat way of pairing the made stitches.

► Work to the yarn-over, then knit into the back of the loop. Drop the second yarn-over off the left needle, then pick it up with the left needle as shown, so that it is turned the other way, and knit into the front of it. The two stitches make a neat inverted V shape over the hole.

WORKING A DOUBLE LIFTED STITCH INCREASE

Knitting into each side of the top of the stitch on the row below makes an increase that's decorative and useful for keeping patterns such as rib and moss stitch correct when shaping. This increase can be varied by knitting into the back of the lifted stitch or purling into the lifted stitch.

◄ Work to the increase, lift the stitch from the row below the next stitch on to the left needle, and knit it. Knit the stitch on the left needle, then lift the stitch previously knitted into on to the left needle, and knit it.

TIP

Use this method to increase just one stitch: knit the lifted stitch, then the next stitch, and the new stitch lies to the right. Knit the stitch, then the lifted stitch, and the increase is on the left.

BIAS AND CHEVRON KNITTING

Use increases and decreases to shape within the fabric of your knitting to create bias and chevron effects.

If you increase and decrease one stitch at opposite ends on alternate rows so that the stitch count remains constant, the knitted fabric will slant while the direction of the stitches remains vertical.

Decreases at the beginning and increases at the end of a row tilt the fabric to the left, increases at the beginning and decreases at the end tilt the fabric to the right. Although often used to make flexible facings, this principle can be used to shape knitted fabrics of any size. The examples shown here are in stockinette stitch – the stripes are used to emphasize the slant – but textured stitch patterns and color motifs can also be shaped in this way. The angle of the slant can be varied by spacing the shapings further apart.

Put left and right bias shapings together to make a chevron fabric with the stitches fanning out from or traveling in to the center. You'll need to work a double increase or decrease at the center – or use single shapings each side of one or more center stitches. A single chevron can be used to create a knitted fabric of any size or you can combine upward and downward pointing chevrons to make stitch patterns.

TIP

Try bias knitting in a stranded color pattern – the motifs will seem to move to the left or right, depending on the shapings.

BIAS KNITTING

To make a flexible bias strip, cast on a few stitches and work the increases and decreases one or two stitches in from each end.

◀ For a slant to the right, increase one stitch at the beginning, and decrease one stitch at the end of each right-side row.

▶ For a slant to the left, decrease one stitch at the beginning and increase one stitch at the end of each right-side row.

CHEVRON KNITTING

These examples are in stockinette with shaping on every right-side row, but you can vary the spacing of the increases and decreases to suit your stitch pattern.

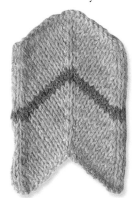

▲ Increasing at each side of the center stitch and decreasing at each end of every right-side row makes the stitches fan out from the center and forms an upward-pointing chevron.

▲ Double decreasing at the center and increasing at each end of every right-side row makes the stitches travel to the center and forms a downward-pointing chevron.

THE STITCH COLLECTION

KNIT AND PURL

Knit-and-purl stitch patterns can be used to create anything from cushions and traditional sweaters to fashion designs in crunchy textures and subtle brocades – the possibilities are endless.

Alternate knit and purl and you get the simplest texture stitches. Group the knits and purls geometrically to make blocks, diagonals, chevrons, and diamonds, or put them together more freely to create motifs. Patterns can be repeated to make an all-over design, or used in panels with simple stitches between. Add interest to knit and purl patterns by knitting into the back of the loops or slipping stitches.

PUTTING KNIT AND PURL TOGETHER

On the right side of the fabric, the knit stitches appear smooth, while each purl stitch makes a little blip. If you think of the smooth stitches as light and the blips as dark, you'll find it easy to read the charts on the following pages.

▲ MOSS STITCH With an odd number of stitches, moss stitch is a one-row pattern. On every row simply knit the first stitch, then purl one, knit one to the end of the row. On an even number of stitches, moss stitch is a two-row pattern (see page 46 for chart).

WORKING INTO THE BACK OF A STITCH

Working into the backs of stitches is often used to add definition to a stitch pattern. It closes up the V shape on the right side of the fabric and makes the diagonals from bottom right to top left more prominent. As the knitting progresses, these diagonals emphasize the verticals on the right side of the fabric.

▲ To knit into the back of a stitch, insert the right needle into the back of the stitch from right to left, take the yarn around the needle and make the new stitch in the usual way.

▲ To purl into the back of a stitch, swing the needle ends slightly away from you to insert the right needle into the back of the stitch from left to right, then take the yarn around the needle and make a new stitch in the usual way.

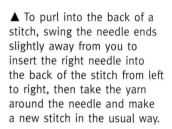

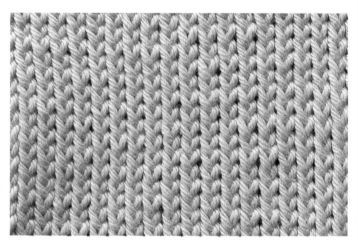

▲ CROSSED STOCKINETTE To work crossed stockinette stitch, knit into the back of each stitch on right-side rows and purl into the back of each stitch on wrong-side rows.

SLIPPING A STITCH

To slip a stitch, simply move it from the left to the right needle without working it. When this is done as part of a stitch pattern, the stitch is usually slipped purlwise, so that the stitch lies on the needle in the same direction as an ordinary knit stitch.

Slipping stitches makes a close, firm fabric. If the stitch is slipped purlwise on a right-side row with the yarn at the back, the design element is vertical. If the stitch is slipped purlwise on a right-side row with the yarn at the front, the design element is horizontal.

Stitches can also be slipped purlwise on wrong-side rows. If the wrong-side row is purled and the yarn is held in front, the strand won't show on the right side; if the yarn is held at the back, the strand will show on the right side.

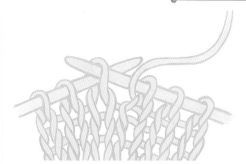

▲ To slip one with yarn in front on a knit row, bring the yarn to the front of the work, insert the right needle into the stitch as if to purl, then slip the stitch from the left to right needle. Take the yarn to back of the work to knit the next stitch.

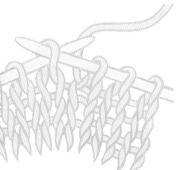

◀ To slip one with yarn at the back on a knit row, insert the right needle into the stitch as if to purl, then slip the stitch from the left to the right needle. Do not take the yarn around the needle – there is no new stitch.

▲ BARRED STOCKINETTE
Purl on wrong side rows, and knit and slip alternately on right-side rows, holding the yarn in front.

Knit and purl stitches alone can make a richly textured design.

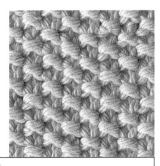

1: MOSS STITCH

2 • • 1

MULTIPLE OF 2 STITCHES PLUS 1

2 • • • 1

MULTIPLE OF 2 STITCHES PLUS 2

2 • • 1

MULTIPLE OF 2 STITCHES PLUS 1

ABOVE
You can start moss stitch with either a knit or a purl stitch.

ABOVE
When working on an even number of stitches, if the first stitch of the first row is knit, the first stitch of the second row will be purl.

2: 3 AND 2 WELTING

LEFT
Welting patterns can be worked on any number of stitches, odd or even, and with any combination of rows of reverse stockinette stitch and stockinette stitch. This fabric spreads widthwise and contracts vertically.

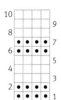

SHOWN OVER 4 STITCHES

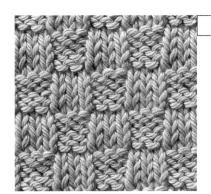

3: LITTLE BLOCKS

LEFT
Patterns of alternating blocks of stockinette stitch and reverse stockinette stitch can be worked over any combination of stitches and rows. Block patterns have a similar gauge to that of stockinette stitch, so the little blocks here appear square even though there are more rows than stitches to each block.

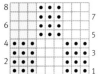

MULTIPLE OF 6 STITCHES PLUS 3

4: BROKEN BLOCKS

ABOVE
Adding a garter ridge to the stockinette stitch blocks makes this pattern look more exciting than plain blocks, yet it's very easy to work.

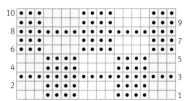

MULTIPLE OF 8 STITCHES PLUS 10

5: DOUBLE MOSS STITCH

MULTIPLE OF 2 STITCHES PLUS 1

6: TINY DOUBLE MOSS DIAMONDS

LEFT
This stitch shows the smallest possible double moss stitch diamonds on stockinette stitch. Use it as an all over pattern, or work just three or four repeats for a textured panel.

MULTIPLE OF 6 STITCHES PLUS 1

ABOVE
Double moss stitch – also called Irish moss – is always a four row pattern, but it can be worked over an odd or an even number of stitches, starting knit or purl as for moss stitch. The chart shows double moss stitch beginning with purl, as this holds the corner of knitting more neatly. If double moss stitch is to be used after p1, k1 rib, then, start with a knit stitch, as in the third row of the chart. Double moss is an extremely useful stitch because the row gauge is similar to that of stockinette stitch, which makes it ideal for creating textured motifs on a stockinette stitch background (see heart and star on page 50).

7: CORNISH LATTICE

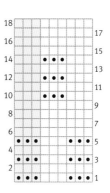

MULTIPLE OF 6 STITCHES PLUS 3

LEFT
This stitch pattern is based on purl garter stitch and stockinette, which makes it easy to work.

8: GARTER DIAMONDS

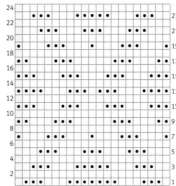

MULTIPLE OF 20 STITCHES PLUS 1

LEFT
Although the large repeat makes this pattern look complicated, it's easy to work because it's made with knit and purl stitches on right-side rows, and every wrong-side row is just purl.

9: TWISTED LITTLE CHECK

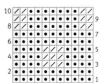

MULTIPLE OF 10 STITCHES PLUS 1

10: TWISTED DIAGONAL

MULTIPLE OF 8 STITCHES PLUS 2

LEFT
You could work the stockinette stitch part of this pattern without twisting the stitches, but the result would be less well-defined diagonals. For a diagonal running to the right, reverse the chart.

FAR LEFT
Working the stockinette stitch squares through the back of the loops gives a lovely definition to the blocks.

11: TWISTED CHEVRON

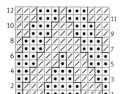

MULTIPLE OF 12 STITCHES PLUS 1

LEFT
When diagonals are worked in alternate directions, they meet to make chevrons. Working stitches through the back of the loops makes the chevrons appear taller and more elegant.

12: TWISTED SQUARE CHECKER

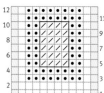

MULTIPLE OF 10 STITCHES PLUS 2

RIGHT
See how the small blocks of stitches, which are worked through the backs of the loops, contrast with the stockinette stitch outlining the blocks.

13: DOUBLE MOSS STITCH STAR

LEFT
This star can be used as a single motif, scattered on a stockinette stitch background, or repeated in blocks. If you're planning to use it as a repeat pattern, chart it out in full to make sure that you have allowed enough extra stockinette stitch background stitches between the stars.

14: DOUBLE MOSS STITCH HEART

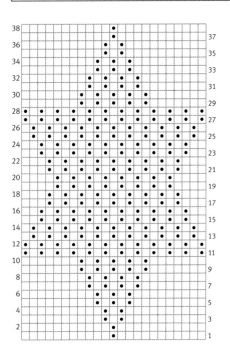

MOTIF OF 23 STITCHES

RIGHT
This heart motif can be used in the same way as the star or combined with other stitch patterns. It's very easy to make this motif larger – simply copy this design onto graph paper, then add more pairs of dots for purl stitches evenly all around the motif until the heart is the size you want.

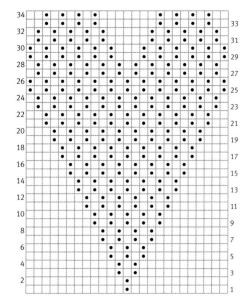

MOTIF OF 25 STITCHES

RIGHT

This densely woven fabric is made by slipping stitches on both right and wrong-side rows. Remember to bring the yarn forward before slipping a stitch on right-side rows and to take the yarn back before slipping a stitch on wrong-side rows, so that the strands always appear on the right side of the work.

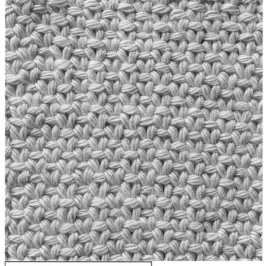

15: LINEN STITCH

MULTIPLE OF 2 STITCHES PLUS 3

RIGHT

Slipping two stitches creates the horizontal strands in this subtle pattern. When you're slipping two stitches, it's easier to slip them purlwise together. Don't strand too tightly, because it will pull in and make a very thick fabric.

16: LITTLE SLIP STITCH HERRINGBONE

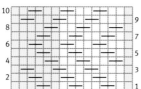

MULTIPLE OF 8 STITCHES PLUS 7

BELOW

Stranded fabrics are not all heavy. In this pattern, also called bowknot, the long strands are linked into a knit stitch to make a lively variation on simple blocks. If you're working the stitch as an all-over pattern on a garment, match the blocks by starting the back as charted. Then for the front, work the first row and start the repeat with the eighth row to alternate the blocks at the side seams.

17: BUTTERFLY BLOCKS

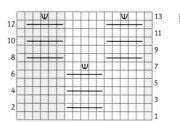

TAKE RIGHT NEEDLE UNDER THE THREE LONG STRANDS AND KNIT THEM WITH THE STITCH.

MULTIPLE OF 10 STITCHES PLUS 7
WORK ROWS 1 TO 13 THEN REPEAT ROWS 2 TO 13

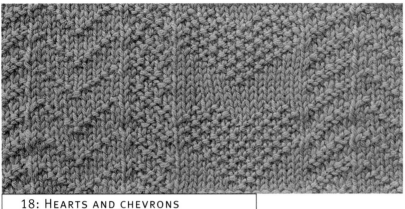

18: Hearts and chevrons

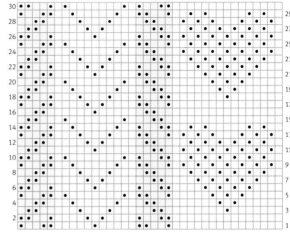

Panel of 5 stitches / 11 stitches / 5 stitches / 15 stitches

ABOVE
Simple knit and purl stitch pattern combinations are typical of Guernsey sweaters. The diagonals, chevrons, and heart patterns given here can all be used as separate panels. The chevron panel is a 10-row repeat, so it fits neatly into the 30-row repeat of the hearts panel. The tiny diagonals repeat every 4 rows, so you'll need to work 60 rows before the pattern repeats exactly.

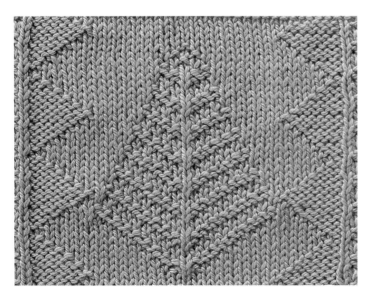

19: Tree and flags

Multiple of 40 stitches plus 1

20: DIAMOND AND NET

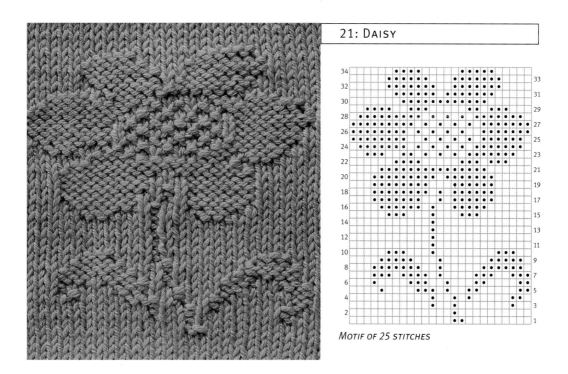

MULTIPLE OF 42 STITCHES PLUS 3

ABOVE

The moss stitch diamond shape is so satisfying because its shape echoes the diamond contained in the criss-cross of the net.

LEFT

Part of the fun in putting panels of stitch patterns together lies in seeing the shapes created between the motifs. Here the interest is heightened by the way the flag panels just miss touching the tree. These Guernsey-type patterns can be used as separate panels or combined with other stitch patterns if you wish. Note that the busy little pattern between the flag panels is simply double moss stitch.

21: DAISY

MOTIF OF 25 STITCHES

ABOVE

Knit and purl stitches can be used to draw naturalistic motifs, using the play of light on the surface of the knitting to define the design. If you want a daisy leaning in the opposite direction, copy the chart onto graph paper in reverse. For a smooth-petaled daisy on a textured background, all you have to do is reverse the knit and purl stitches.

RIB

Simple ribs are combinations of knit and purl stitches that form verticals which pull the knitting in across the width.

In rib, the knit stitches are raised and the purl stitches sink down. The resulting elasticity makes rib very suitable for edgings and cuffs. Some ribbed garments are designed to fit closely, however, choice of yarn is important. Wool, for example, will make a springy, stretchy rib, while cotton ribs will lie flat. In the wrong yarn, a skinny rib sweater just won't cling.

Ribs are usually worked on needles one, two, or more sizes smaller than for other stitches. The smaller the needle size, the more the rib will contract. Interesting patterns can be made by combining simple rib with cable, lace, and twist stitches.

Measuring the length of a piece of ribbing can be difficult, since this measurement will vary depending on whether the knitting is stretched or contracted widthwise. In the end, it's best to measure ribs half stretched unless the instructions state otherwise.

AN ASSORTMENT OF STITCH HOLDERS.

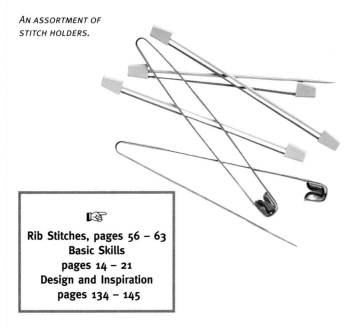

☞
Rib Stitches, pages 56 – 63
Basic Skills
pages 14 – 21
Design and Inspiration
pages 134 – 145

SINGLE RIB

For this basic rib, alternate knit and purl stitches are worked above each other.

▶Over an even number of stitches repeat k1, p1 to the end of the row. The second row is the same. Over an odd number of stitches, begin k1, then p1, k1 to the end. On alternate rows begin p1, then k1, p1 to the end.

DOUBLE RIB

Knit two, purl two rib makes a very elastic fabric with strongly defined ridges and furrows.

◀This rib can be worked on a number of stitches divisible by four, in which case k2, p2 is repeated along each row. To balance it at each end, work on a number of stitches divisible by four, plus two. The first row begins k2 and is followed by p2, k2 repeated to the end. The second row begins p2, followed by k2, p2 to the end.

BROKEN RIB

This variation on double rib does not pull in.

RIB VARIATIONS

Fisherman's rib is an interesting variation on knit one, purl one rib. Knitting alternate stitches in the row below gives a deeper, softer rib. Brioche rib looks similar, but it uses no purl stitches. It's made with slipped stitches and yarn overs. Detailed instructions are charted on page 63.

▶FISHERMAN'S RIB

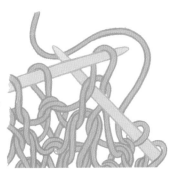

To knit in the row below, the stitch is knitted in the usual way, except that the point of the right needle goes into the stitch directly underneath the first stitch on the left needle. Both strands are then dropped off the needle together.

RIB CARDIGAN
Rib stitch can give a garment elasticity and a flattering body-hugging shape.

▶BRIOCHE RIB

When knitting together a slipped stitch and a yarn-over, the two strands are already in place on the needle and are knitted together in the usual way.

1: KNIT ONE PURL, ONE RIB

MULTIPLE OF 2 STITCHES PLUS 1

ABOVE
As the name suggests, alternate knit and purl stitches make up this rib. It's also called single rib or one-and-one rib.

2: BROKEN SINGLE RIB

MULTIPLE OF 2 STITCHES PLUS 1

LEFT
Purling the wrong-side rows reduces the elasticity of the rib and produces an attractive texture.

3: SINGLE TWISTED RIB

MULTIPLE OF 2 STITCHES PLUS 1

LEFT
This well-defined rib has the knit stitches on the right side and the purl stitches on the wrong side worked through the back of the loop.

4: KNIT TWO, PURL TWO RIB

MULTIPLE OF 4 STITCHES PLUS 2

LEFT
Also known as
double rib or two-
and-two rib, this
classic stitch is the
same on both sides.

BELOW
Interrupting k2, p2
rib with small bands
of welting makes an
interesting variation
on a familiar theme.

6: BAMBOO RIB

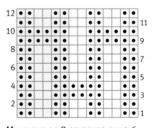

MULTIPLE OF 8 STITCHES PLUS 6

LEFT
Purling wrong-side
rows turns k2, p2
into a firm fabric
with verticals of
stockinette stitch and
garter stitch.

5: BROKEN DOUBLE RIB

MULTIPLE OF 4 STITCHES PLUS 2

RIGHT
Panels of diagonal ribs are made with increases and decreases.

BELOW
Moving k2, p2 ribs along one stitch on alternate rows produces well-defined diagonals.

8: TILTED RIB

MULTIPLE OF 42 STITCHES PLUS 8

▽   PURL INTO THE FRONT OF THE STITCH, THEN K INTO BACK OF THE STITCH

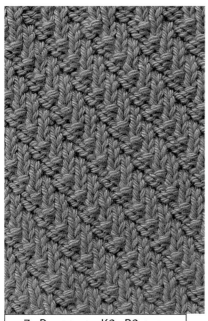

7: DIAGONAL K2, P2 RIB

MULTIPLE OF 4 STITCHES

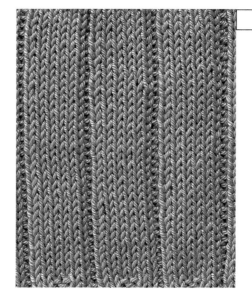

9: WIDE RIB

MULTIPLE OF 8 STITCHES PLUS 2

LEFT
A wide rib can comprise any number of stitches. This one combines six of stockinette stitch with two of reverse stockinette stitch.

LEFT
Joining up single ribs with small blocks of welting makes an allover diagonal pattern.

RIGHT
Knitting a stitch through the back of the loop on right-side rows throws up a neat little blip on a reverse stockinette stitch ground.

10: **Welted rib**

11: **Shadow rib**

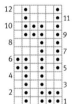

MULTIPLE OF 6 STITCHES

2 • • • • •
 • • • / • • 1

MULTIPLE OF 3 STITCHES PLUS 2

12: **Close stitch**

1 • • • 2

MULTIPLE OF 2 STITCHES PLUS 1

RIGHT
Slipped stitches make this gentle rib very thick and soft.

RIGHT
This ribbed stitch is
used to reinforce sock
and stocking heels.

13: STOCKING HEEL RIB

MULTIPLE OF 2 STITCHES PLUS 1

BELOW
Slipping stitches on
both sides of the
knitting gives well-
defined ridges and a
fabric that is the same
on both sides.

BELOW
Moss stitch panels
make this slip stitch
rib extra firm and
substantial.

14: MOSS AND SLIP STITCH RIB

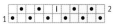

MULTIPLE OF 6 STITCHES PLUS 5

15: CARTRIDGE BELT RIB

MULTIPLE OF 4 STITCHES PLUS 3

16: MOSS RIB

MULTIPLE OF 6 STITCHES PLUS 1

LEFT
Another reversible
stitch, this combines
single rib and moss
stitch.

BELOW
This firm rib combines
stitches worked through
the back of the loop
with a nubbly knit and
purl texture.

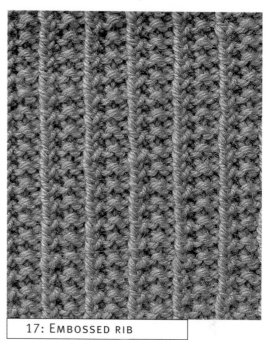

17: EMBOSSED RIB

MULTIPLE OF 4 STITCHES PLUS 3

18: BROKEN MOSS RIB

MULTIPLE OF 10 STITCHES PLUS 3

LEFT
Dividing stockinette
stitch panels with
moss stitch gives a
flat, mock rib.

LEFT
Panels of double moss stitch alternate with k1, p1 rib.

RIGHT
Although it looks like a twisted rib, this effect is achieved by taking a slipped stitch over an increase.

20: CROSSED RIB

19: DOUBLE MOSS RIB

MULTIPLE OF 6 STITCHES PLUS 1

MULTIPLE OF 3 STITCHES PLUS 1

SL 1 ST KNITWISE, K IN FRONT AND BACK OF NEXT ST, PSSO.

21: DOUBLE MOSS DIAMOND RIB

MULTIPLE OF 10 STITCHES PLUS 3

LEFT
Both sides of this rib are attractive. On the reverse, the diamonds sit on a stockinette stitch background and the ribs are less conspicuous.

22: FISHERMAN'S RIB

MULTIPLE OF 2 STITCHES PLUS 3

AFTER WORKING ROW 1, REPEAT ONLY ROWS 2 AND 3

Ⓥ   *KNIT IN THE ROW BELOW*

LEFT
Knitting alternate stitches in the row below is the secret of this deep, soft rib. Both sides look the same.

RIGHT
This rib looks similar to fisherman's rib but is made quite differently.

23: BRIOCHE RIB

MULTIPLE OF 2 STITCHES PLUS 3

Θ   *YFWD, SL 1 ST PURLWISE, TAKE YARN OVER NEEDLE.*

△   *K TOG THE SL ST AND THE YO.*

CABLES

Knitting groups of stitches out of sequence creates some of the world's most exciting stitch patterns. Cables can be worked with two or more stitches, and they can be crossed to the front or the back to make hundreds of coiling and interlacing stitch patterns.

Cable stitches are traditionally associated with Aran sweaters, in which rich panels of ropes, plaits, diamonds, trellis, and embossed stitches are combined to flamboyant effect. Contemporary designers often combine cable stitches to make fascinating figurative motifs. Classic cables are more restrained and give a sophisticated touch to even the plainest garment.

Once you understand the following techniques, you'll find it easy to customize basic cables, making them wider or taller, cabling more frequently for a firmer fabric, or less often for a softer effect.

HOW TO CABLE

When one, two, or more stitches are cabled, a short double-pointed needle is used to transfer the stitches. When the cable needle is held at the back, the stitches on the right side of the work make a diagonal from left to right. When the cable needle is held at the front, the stitches make a diagonal from right to left. Cable stitches can be knitted, purled, or textured as given in the pattern instructions. Once you've mastered the techniques for basic four-stitch cables, you will be able to tackle any of the stitches in this section.

▼ ROPES AND WAVES

In the center, front and back cables repeat to make ropes, while at each side they alternate to make waves.

BACK CABLE

This four-stitch cable crosses at the back and has all the stitches knitted.

1 Slip the first two stitches on to a cable needle and hold at the back of the work, then knit the next two stitches from the left needle.

2 Knit the two stitches from the cable needle.

FRONT CABLE

All the stitches are knitted, but this four-stitch cable crosses at the front.

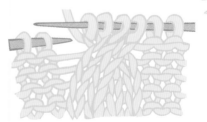

1 Slip the first two stitches on to a cable needle and hold at the front of the work, then knit the next two stitches from the left needle.

2 Knit the two stitches from the cable needle.

▶ HONEYCOMB/ZIGZAG

Knit and purl four-stitch cables are used to make these patterns.

BACK PURL CABLE

Here's how to work a four-stitch cable with knit stitches moving to the right on a purl background – called c4bp.

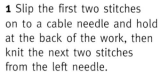

1 Slip the first two stitches on to a cable needle and hold at the back of the work, then knit the next two stitches from the left needle.

2 Purl the two stitches from the cable needle.

FRONT PURL CABLE

Here's how to work a four-stitch cable with knit stitches making a diagonal to the left on a purl background.

1 Slip the first two stitches on to a cable needle and hold at the front of work, then purl the next two stitches from the left needle.

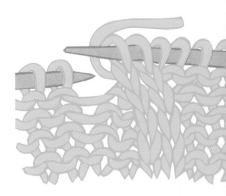

2 Knit the two stitches from the cable needle.

 TIP

Counting rows between cables can be tricky. Slip a marker of contrast yarn between stitches on the cable row and pull it out afterwards.

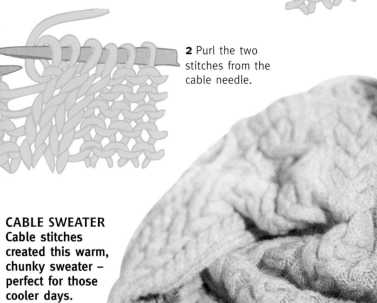

CABLE SWEATER
Cable stitches created this warm, chunky sweater – perfect for those cooler days.

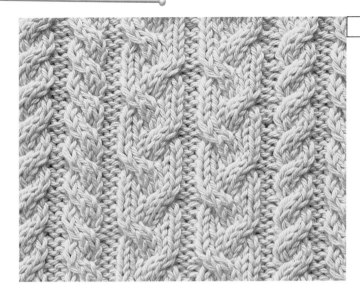

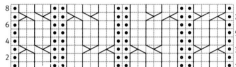

1: PLAITS AND ROPES

MULTIPLE OF 28 STITCHES

ABOVE
Little cables worked over four rows are fine on their own but are especially good for slipping in between bigger panels. Here they're used with eight-row plaits.

RIGHT
This panel is surprisingly easy to work, because all the wrong-side rows are just purl. There's no limit to the number of strands you can plait – just add six more stitches for each strand.

2: FOUR-STRAND PLAIT AND SNAKE CABLES

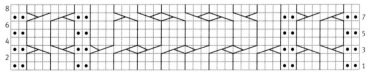

PANEL OF 44 STITCHES

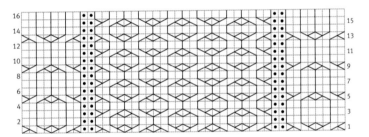

3: OXO AND HONEYCOMB

PANEL OF 44 STITCHES

BELOW
The easy three-over-three cables at the top of each block make this simple pattern of knit and purl blocks look more complicated than it really is.

4: CABLE CHECK

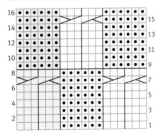

MULTIPLE OF 12 STITCHES PLUS 6

ABOVE
The center panel of honeycomb cable has a repeat of eight stitches, so you could work it over any multiple of eight to make it wider or narrower.

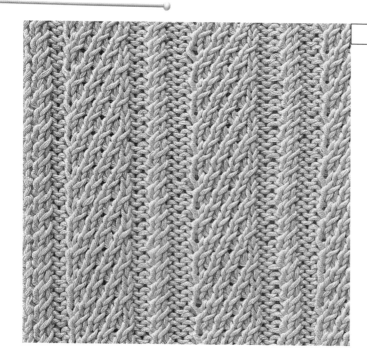

5: LITTLE CABLE RIBS

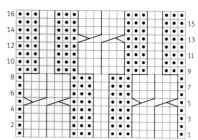

MULTIPLE OF 13 STITCHES PLUS 6

LEFT

Two-stitch crosses are often twisted, but the smooth effect created by true cabling is worth the extra work, as this pattern shows. You could make the spiral rib wider by adding any multiple of two stitches.

RIGHT

Here a six-stitch-wide cable alternates with a two-stitch rib. The pattern looks very busy, but it's easy to do.

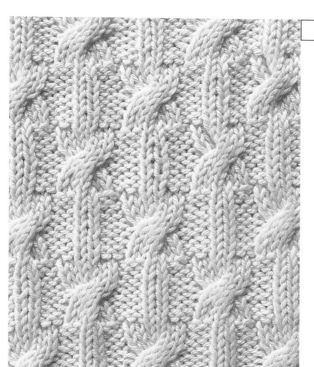

6: CABLE KNOT RIB

MULTIPLE OF 14 STITCHES PLUS 8

7: PLAIT AND RIB

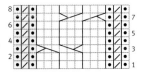

MULTIPLE OF 12 STITCHES PLUS 3

LEFT
If you'd like a fatter plait, try working over twelve stitches, cabling four over four each time.

RIGHT
Two-over-two cables along the edges of stockinette stitch panels contrast effectively with narrow bands of garter stitch. All wrong-side rows are purled.

8: DECKLE EDGE

MULTIPLE OF 12 STITCHES PLUS 2

9: TRIPLE ZIGZAG AND ROPE

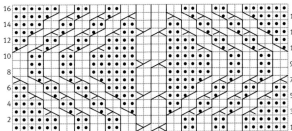

PANEL OF 36 STITCHES

LEFT
This zigzag is the same as the one on page 65, but it looks a lot more interesting in a group of three. Reverse the rope cable if you're working a pair of panels.

10: TWO-TEXTURE ZIGZAG

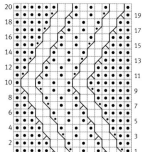

MULTIPLE OF 14 STITCHES PLUS 2

LEFT
This pattern is a good one for getting used to knit and purl cables, because the purl stitch always fits into the double moss stitch. To reverse the zigzag, start the chart on the 11th row.

11: SMOCKED CABLE

PANEL OF 24 STITCHES

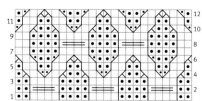

K4, SL ALL 4 STS ONTO CABLE NEEDLE AND HOLD AT FRONT. WIND YARN TIGHTLY COUNTER-CLOCKWISE AROUND STS ON CABLE NEEDLE 4 TIMES, ENDING AT WRONG SIDE. SL 4 STS BACK ON TO RIGHT NEEDLE.

LEFT
Although smocking can be created by sewing ribs together, using cables and clusters gives better definition.

12: TEXTURED CABLE

LEFT
Moss stitch is the texture used in this six-stitch cable, but k1, p1 rib could be substituted, with the knit stitches worked through the back of the loops.

RIGHT
These cabled leaves are used here for an allover pattern, but they could also be combined with other cable stitches.

13: LEAF CABLE

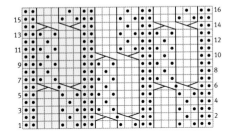

MULTIPLE OF 16 STITCHES PLUS 10

 SL 3 STS ONTO CABLE NEEDLE AND HOLD AT FRONT, K3, THEN K1, P1, K1 FROM CABLE NEEDLE.

 SL 3 STS ONTO CABLE NEEDLE AND HOLD AT FRONT, K1, P1, K1, THEN K3 FROM CABLE NEEDLE.

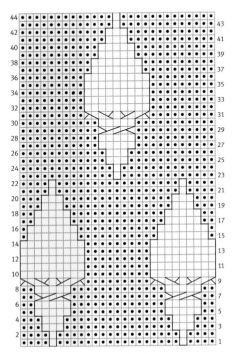

MULTIPLE OF 18 STITCHES PLUS 9

RIGHT
Extra cables springing out of the background add interest to an allover trellis pattern.

BELOW
Using crossed stitches gives this enclosed rope cable lots of character.

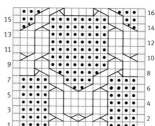

14: HORSESHOE TRELLIS

MULTIPLE OF 16 STITCHES PLUS 2

BELOW
One-over-one cables and stitches crossed by working through the back of the loop form stylized flowers.

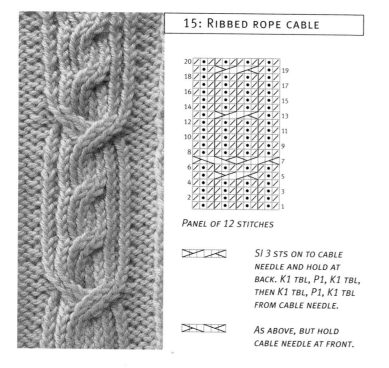

15: RIBBED ROPE CABLE

PANEL OF 12 STITCHES

SI 3 STS ON TO CABLE NEEDLE AND HOLD AT BACK. K1 TBL, P1, K1 TBL, THEN K1 TBL, P1, K1 TBL FROM CABLE NEEDLE.

AS ABOVE, BUT HOLD CABLE NEEDLE AT FRONT.

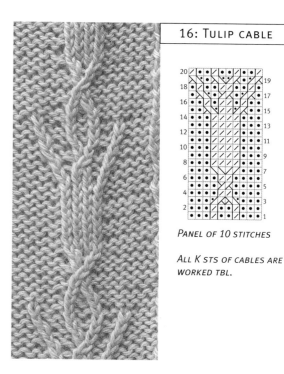

16: TULIP CABLE

PANEL OF 10 STITCHES

ALL K STS OF CABLES ARE WORKED TBL.

RIGHT

Elegant curves can be made with very simple cables. This stitch pattern can be used as a panel, or staggered, as a repeat.

17: BROCADE

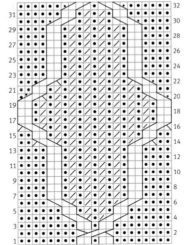

PANEL OF 21 STITCHES

SL NEXT 2 STS ONTO CABLE NEEDLE AND HOLD AT BACK, K2, THEN P1, K1 TBL FROM CABLE NEEDLE.

SL NEXT 2 STS ONTO CABLE NEEDLE AND HOLD AT FRONT, K1 TBL, P1, THEN K2 FROM CABLE NEEDLE.

RIGHT

Cabling on wrong-side rows is no harder than cabling on the right side. And because the stitches from the four-stitch cable are cabled again on the next row, they spring out cleanly giving lovely oval shapes.

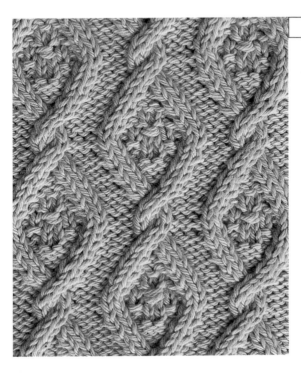

18: OVALS AND FLOWERS

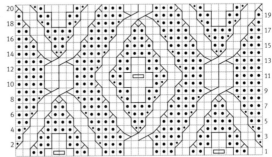

PANEL OF 34 STITCHES

K2, SL THESE 2 STS ONTO CABLE NEEDLE AND HOLD AT FRONT. WIND YARN COUNTER-CLOCK-WISE AROUND STS ON CABLE NEEDLE 3 TIMES, ENDING AT WRONG SIDE. SL 2 STS BACK ONTO RIGHT NEEDLE.

C3BP AND   C3FP ARE WORKED ON WS ROWS.

TWISTS

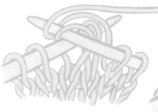

Twisting stitches is working two or three stitches out of sequence, but without using a cable needle. This is an easy way to create patterns where lines of stitches travel over the surface of the knitting.

Some twist stitch patterns look like miniature cables, others create diagonals, zig zags, and diamonds. Twisting stitches closes up the work, so densely twisted stitched patterns can make the fabric thicker and less flexible – unless larger needles are used.

Twists are sometimes combined with cable stitch patterns with the shallower twists complementing the depths of the cables. The advantage of twist stitches is that they can be worked more quickly than cable stitches.

Although twists are easy to do, there are lots of tiny but important variations that change the appearance of a twist.

They can be worked on right- or wrong-side rows, and the stitches can be all knit, all purl, or a combination of the two. Twist stitch patterns are easy to work in the round from a chart – especially the patterns that move a stitch on every row. Simply read every row of the chart from right to left, interpreting all the symbols as right-side-row twists.

☞
**Twist Stitches pages 76 – 83
Design and Inspiration
pages 134 – 145
Gallery pages 146 – 155**

HOW TO WORK A LEFT TWIST

This twist is worked on a right side row. As the stitches change place, the first stitch lies on top and slants to the left, while the stitch behind is worked through the back of the loop.

1 Knit into the back of the second stitch.

2 Knit into the front of the first stitch.

3 Slip both stitches off the left needle together.

LEFT TWIST VARIATIONS

To work a knit-and-purl two-stitch twist slanting to the left, purl into the back of the second stitch, then knit into the front of the first stitch. To twist two stitches to the left on a wrong side row, purl into the back of the second stitch, then purl into the front of the first stitch.

HOW TO WORK A RIGHT TWIST

In this right-sided row twist, the second stitch lies on top and slants to the right, while the stitch behind is worked through the back of the loop.

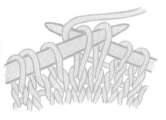 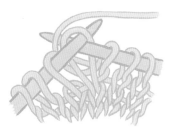

1 Knit into the front of the second stitch.

2 Knit into the back of the first stitch.

3 Slip both stitches off the left needle together.

HERRINGBONE TWIST

▶ This twist pattern uses left and right twists on a stockinette stitch background, but the top stitches of the twists are made more prominent by slipping them on wrong-side rows.

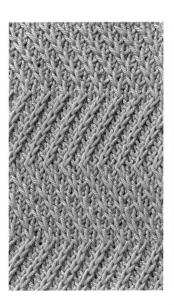

TWISTS SWEATER
A stone-wash effect gives this cotton sweater an extra dimension.

RIGHT TWIST VARIATIONS

There are two other ways of working this knit twist. Either knit into the front instead of the back of the first stitch in Step 2. Or knit two together, then knit the first stitch again before slipping the stitches off the left needle. To work a knit-and-purl right twist, knit into the front of the second stitch, then purl the first stitch. To twist two stitches to the right on a wrong side row, purl into the front of the second stitch, then into the front of the first stitch.

1: HERRINGBONE TWIST

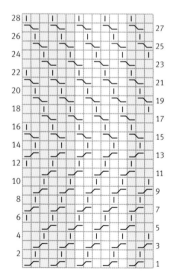

MULTIPLE OF 6 STITCHES PLUS 3

ABOVE
Shown on page 75.

2: TINY TRELLIS

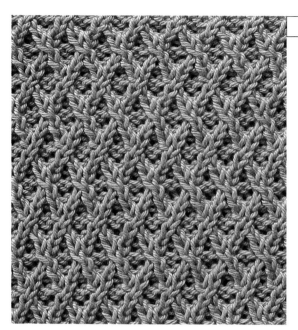

MULTIPLE OF 4 STITCHES PLUS 2

LEFT
If worked over 10 stitches, this pattern makes a crossed diamond panel.

LEFT
Use this pattern as an interesting alternative to rib; simply plan more purl stitches between plaits to suit your design.

3: MINIATURE PLAIT

MULTIPLE OF 4 STITCHES PLUS 1

4: BRANCHED RIB

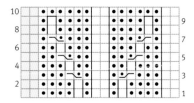

MULTIPLE OF 16 STITCHES PLUS 2

5: BELLFLOWER BLOCKS

MULTIPLE OF 8 STITCHES PLUS 6

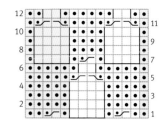 P INTO FRONT OF 2ND ST ON LEFT-HAND NEEDLE THEN INTO FRONT OF FIRST ST, SL BOTH STS OFF NEEDLE TOG.

FAR LEFT

This decorated rib doesn't pull in very much, so can be used as an allover pattern. If you want all the branches to twist in the same direction, repeat the first or last eight stitches of the chart.

LEFT

Simply twisting the stitches at the top of each block produces this pretty pattern. See bellflower motif on page 83 for another use of these blocks.

RIGHT

Twist stitches are good for giving an Aran effect in miniature.

6: WAVE AND TWIST

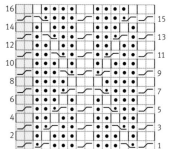

MULTIPLE OF 14 STITCHES PLUS 2

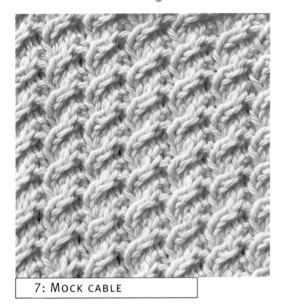

7: MOCK CABLE

MULTIPLE OF 8 STITCHES PLUS 1

RIGHT
Simple twist stitches on the right side and purl rows on the wrong side make an easy stitch with plenty of texture.

LEFT
This attractive pattern is easier than it looks. It uses three-stitch twists.

8: MOCK CABLE 2

MULTIPLE OF 5 STITCHES PLUS 2

RIGHT
For a three-twist lattice simply work rows one and two twice, then rows three to 10. Work rows 11 and 12 twice, then rows 13 to 20, making a 24-row repeat.
For a wider lattice, work on a multiple of 10 stitches, allowing two more purl stitches between twists on the first row, then moving the stitches four times to create the diamond shapes.

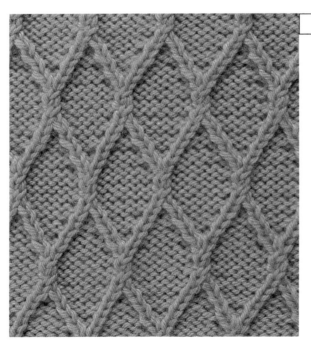

9: TWO-TWIST LATTICE

MULTIPLE OF 8 STITCHES PLUS 2

RIGHT

Slipping the traveling stitches on wrong-side rows makes them lie smoothly; and because they're stretched over two rows, they can be seen clearly even though the background is stockinette stitch.

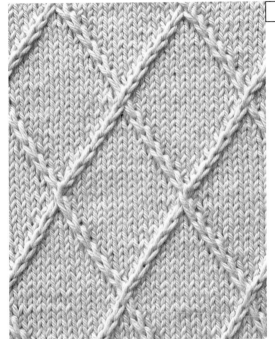

10: Slip-stitch lattice

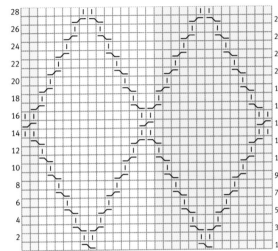

MULTIPLE OF 14 STITCHES PLUS 2

RIGHT

Twisting together two stitches on every row makes a firm, well-defined rib.

11: Twisted rib

MULTIPLE OF 4 STITCHES PLUS 2

(WS) P INTO FRONT OF 2ND ST ON LEFT-HAND NEEDLE, P INTO FIRST ST, SL BOTH STS OFF NEEDLE TOG.

BELOW
Stockinette stitch zigzags are outlined with twisted stitches for more definition and surface texture.

RIGHT
The twisted stitches inside the inverted pyramids could be cabled, but twisting them gives a smoother texture.

13: INVERTED PYRAMIDS

12: ZIGZAGS

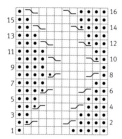

MULTIPLE OF 12 STITCHES

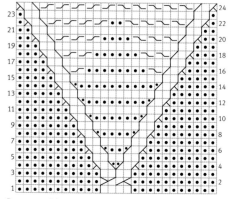

PANEL OF 26 STITCHES

14: SLIP STITCH DIAGONALS

MULTIPLE OF 16 STITCHES PLUS 7

LEFT
Slipping the traveling stitches on the previous row elongates and gives extra definition to these diagonals and ribs.

RIGHT
Slipping stitches on wrong side rows beneath the twist gives a graceful curve to oval mock cables.

15: SLIP STITCH OVALS

MULTIPLE OF 12 STITCHES PLUS 8

16: TWIST STITCH BAND

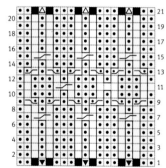

MULTIPLE OF 6 STITCHES PLUS 13 (CAST ON
A MULTIPLE OF 4 STITCHES PLUS 9)

▼   INCREASE 2 STS BY WORKING [K1,
     YO, K1] IN ST.

◭   DECREASE 2 STS: SSK, THEN SL
     REM ST BACK ON TO LEFT NEEDLE
     AND SL 2ND ST ON NEEDLE OVER.

LEFT
This band appears to
sit on the surface of
the knitting because
of the increases in
the first row and the
decreases in the last
row.

RIGHT
Slipped traveling
stitches make a
skeleton leaf pattern
against a subtle knit-
and-purl textured
shape.

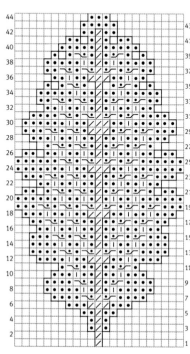

17: OAK LEAF

MOTIF OF 23 STITCHES

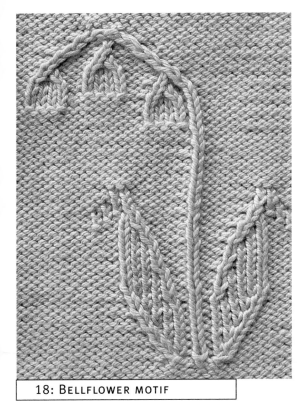

18: BELLFLOWER MOTIF

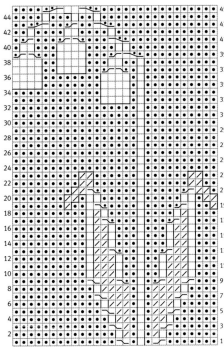

MOTIF OF 28 STITCHES

LEFT
Of course you can't really knit stitches horizontally! You'll need to embroider two chain stitches to complete the curve at the top of the stem when you've finished knitting. The rest of the motif is surprisingly simple.

RIGHT
You'll find this 20-row repeat quite easy to follow, even though you do need to watch out for twists on the wrong-side rows.

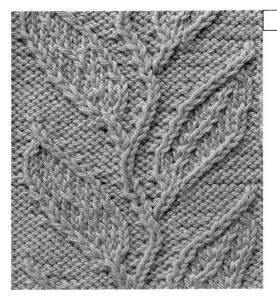

19: BRANCHING LEAVES

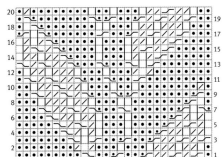

PANEL OF 27 STITCHES

LACE

Lace stitch patterns are simply a combination of decreases and open increases. The new stitches are made by taking the yarn over the needle, to create a light and airy effect.

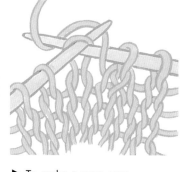

The easiest lace patterns have each increase worked next to the corresponding decrease, so the stitch count stays the same on every row. In other patterns, the increases and decreases occur at different places along the row, but you'll find these just as easy to work as the total number of stitches on each row doesn't change. For some beautiful laces, the increases and decreases are made on different rows, making it harder to keep track of the stitch count, but creating exquisite patterns.

Your choice of yarn will affect the appearance of your lace knitting. Firm, smooth yarns will make the construction more visible; soft or brushed yarns will blur the pattern. Traditionally, very fine wool or cotton is worked on relatively large needles. When the work is pressed, the delicate texture of the lace is revealed.

MAKING A YARN-OVER

It's essential to take the yarn over the needle so that the strand lies in the same direction as the other stitches. Working into this strand on the next row makes a hole, but if the strand is twisted, the hole will close up. When the stitch before a yarn-over is purl, the yarn will already be at the front, ready to go over the needle.

◄ To make a yarn-over between knit stitches; bring the yarn to the front as if to purl, take it over the needle to knit the next stitch.

► To make a yarn-over between knit and purl; bring the yarn to the front as if to purl, take it over the needle, and bring it to the front again, ready to purl.

SIMPLE ALL-OVER FAGGOT LACE

A very open mesh texture is made over an even number of stitches by working yarn over, knit two stitches together along every row.

MAKING MULTIPLE YARN-OVERS

Some lace patterns have larger holes made by working two or more yarn-overs together. The extra yarn-overs may be dropped on the following row, so that only one stitch is increased, or they may all be worked so that several stitches are made.

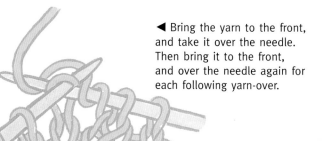

◄ Bring the yarn to the front, and take it over the needle. Then bring it to the front, and over the needle again for each following yarn-over.

CREATING LACE PATTERNS

Using the same decreases with yarn-over increases but placing them next to each other or spacing them apart creates quite different effects.

► Here, the decreases are worked immediately to one side of the yarn-overs, outlining the zig zags.

▼ This zig zag has the decrease separated from the yarn-overs, so that they form gently wandering lines up the fabric.

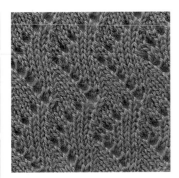

▲ The steep angle of these chevrons is the result of patterning on alternate rows.

TIP

When knitting a garment, don't confuse the increases or decreases of the shapings with the increases and decreases of the lace stitch pattern – or the stitch count made by the shapings will be incorrect.

LACE TOP AND SCARF
Fine yarns have been used to great effect for these examples of Shetland lace knitting.

Working increases and decreases only on right-side rows creates a different effect from patterning on every row.

► Here, the patterning is on every row, giving a lacier appearance as well as a less sharply angled chevron.

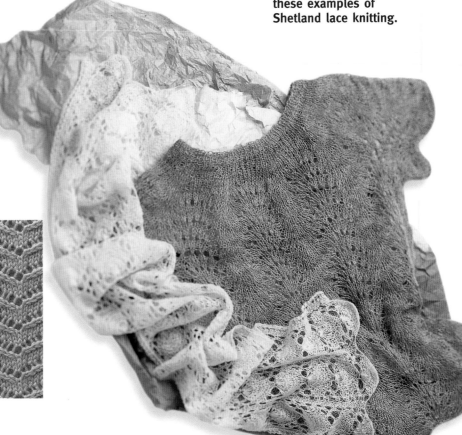

1: FEATHER AND FAN

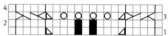

MULTIPLE OF 14 STITCHES PLUS 1

◩ *K4 TOG*

◪ *SL 2 STS KNITWISE, K2 TOG TBL,
PASS SL STS OVER*

LEFT
This is an old
Shetland lace stitch
with many variations.
Common to them all
is the grouping of
increases and
decreases separately
along the row to
make patterns
resembling feathers,
fans, waves, and
scallops.

RIGHT
Cables have been
added to this Feather
and Fan pattern.
Some of the
decreases are worked
two rows away from
the increases,
resulting in a
different row count
in pairs of rows.

2: CABLED FEATHER

MULTIPLE OF 19 STITCHES PLUS 2

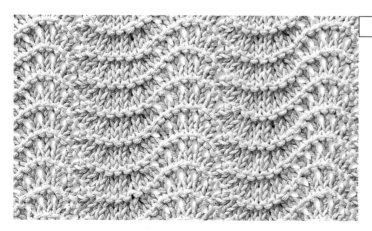

3: OLD SHALE

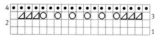

MULTIPLE OF 18 STITCHES PLUS 1

LEFT
This version of a
famous Shetland lace
stitch is particularly
simple and rhythmic.

4: SMALL HEARTS

ABOVE

These two simple hearts could be used as repeat patterns or scattered among other motifs.

MOTIF OF 13 STITCHES

MOTIF OF 11 STITCHES

△ *K2 TOG, RETURN ST TO LEFT NEEDLE, PASS NEXT ST OVER IT, SL ST BACK ON TO RIGHT NEEDLE*

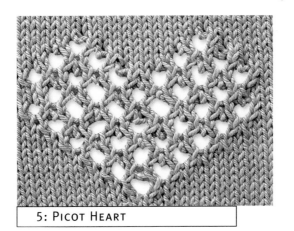

5: PICOT HEART

MOTIF OF 24 STITCHES

LEFT

The double eyelets that make this heart have themselves a heart shape, made by working p1, k1 into the double yarn-over, instead of the usual k1, p1.

BELOW

Yarn-over increases and their corresponding decreases help to shape this heart as well as decorate it.

6: PIERCED HEART

MOTIF OF 21 STITCHES

BELOW
Cabling a faggot rib creates a stitch that can be used as an allover repeat or in conjunction with other open stitches.

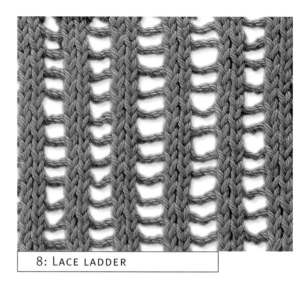

8: Lace ladder

LEFT
Very smooth and controlled, this ladder is quite stable in spite of its open texture.

MULTIPLE OF 4 STITCHES PLUS 2

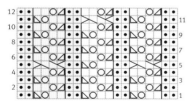

7: Scotch faggot cable

MULTIPLE OF 12 STITCHES PLUS 8

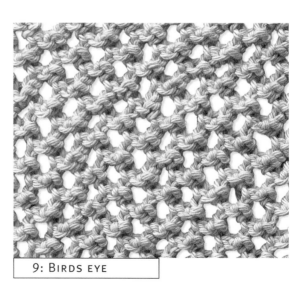

9: Birds eye

LEFT
Allover double eyelets make an unusually textured lace pattern.

MULTIPLE OF 4 STITCHES PLUS 4

BELOW

Bobbles are very
compatible with
many lace stitches.
Here, clusters of
bobbles have been
added to a leaf stitch.

10: LEAVES AND BERRIES

PANEL OF 21 STITCHES PLUS 2

⬤ = [K1, P1, K1, P1, K1] IN NEXT ST, TURN, P5, TURN, SL
2ND, 3RD, 4TH, 5TH STS IN SEQUENCE OVER FIRST ST,
K ST TBL

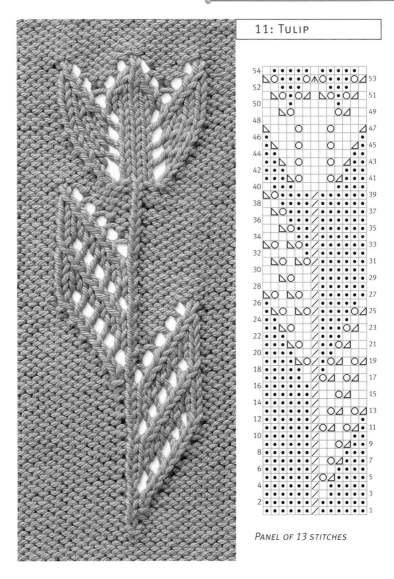

11: TULIP

PANEL OF 13 STITCHES

ABOVE

Many pictorial effects
can be achieved with
lace stitches – this
tulip is slightly
embossed.

BELOW
This simple but sophisticated panel would work well alongside cables.

13: CANDLELIGHT

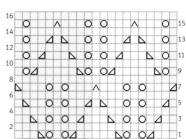

MULTIPLE OF 10 STITCHES PLUS 11

ABOVE
Lace knitting lends itself to flame- and leaf-like patterns. In each of these motifs, the decreases move away from the increases, pulling the stitches into outlines.

BELOW
This pattern is similar to Candlelight in construction, but the decreases pull the stitches in to form the central vein of each leaf.

14: FALLING LEAVES

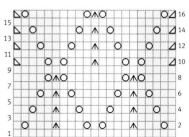

MULTIPLE OF 10 STITCHES PLUS 11

12: DIAMOND SPIRAL

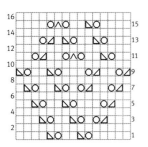

PANEL OF 15 STITCHES

15: PAIRED LEAVES

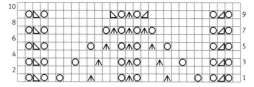

PANEL OF 29 STITCHES

ABOVE
The increases and decreases form drooping leaves with veins and make the lower edge strongly shaped.

RIGHT
Here, increases outline long, feather-like shapes.

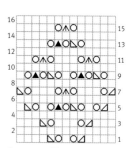

16: CLUSTERED LEAVES

PANEL OF 13 STITCHES

▲ K3 TOG

LEFT
Repeating all 16 rows of this chart makes an attractive panel. A single repeat makes a large motif, or one of the leaves can easily be adapted to make a tiny motif.

17: FEATHER LACE

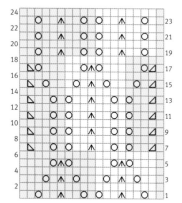

MULTIPLE OF 8 STITCHES PLUS 3

RIGHT

This is a progression of Feather Lace. One repeat of the chart makes a border, while repeating rows 1 to 16 produces an allover pattern.

18: GOTHIC LACE

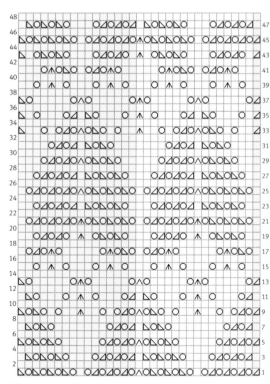

MULTIPLE OF 8 STITCHES PLUS 1

RIGHT

Despite the background being very open, this isn't a difficult stitch to knit. But note the use of two different double decreases.

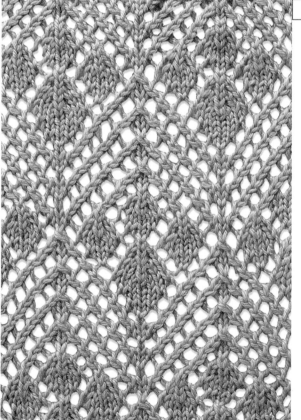

19: LEAF CASCADE

MULTIPLE OF 16 STITCHES PLUS 17

RIGHT

This leafy edging in garter stitch has large eyelets made with multiple yarn-overs.

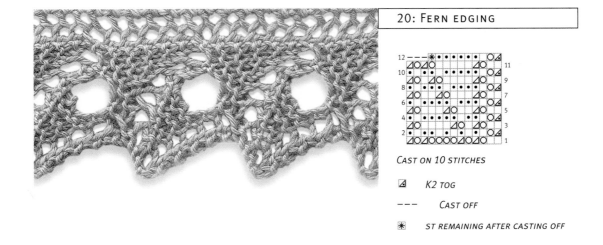

20: FERN EDGING

CAST ON 10 STITCHES

◿   K2 TOG

---   CAST OFF

✳   ST REMAINING AFTER CASTING OFF

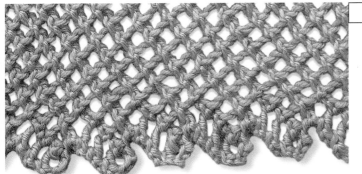

21: MESH LACE EDGING

CAST ON 14 STITCHES

---   CAST OFF

✳   ST REMAINING AFTER CASTING OFF

LEFT

As the pattern is based on garter stitch, either side can be used as the right side. This picture shows the smooth side.

RIGHT

This is a classic edging which has many uses. It repays careful pressing to open out the lace.

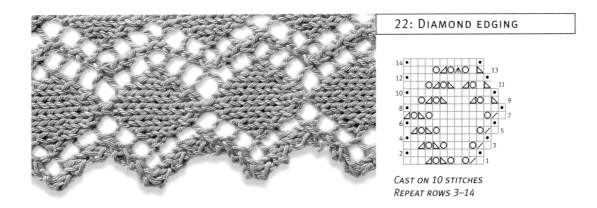

22: DIAMOND EDGING

CAST ON 10 STITCHES
REPEAT ROWS 3–14

BOBBLES AND LEAVES

By using increases and decreases, you can embellish the surface of your knitting with three-dimensional stitches, creating a variety of interesting effects.

A group of increased stitches, decreased abruptly, makes a knot or a bobble which can be used to add emphasis to a familiar cable or lace pattern.

Knots are worked into one stitch and completed without turning the work. Bobbles are also worked into one stitch but have extra rows added by turning and working the bobble stitches only. Different size bobbles can be scattered or clustered according to the design. Bobbles, knots, and leaves are often worked on a reverse stockinette background to emphasize the contrast.

Larger groups of decorative increases and decreases worked over several rows make a blister – a flat, raised shape – or a leaf which can be used as part of a motif or be integrated into a stitch pattern.

There is also a family of all-over textured popcorn and blackberry stitches that are made from repeated groups of increases and decreases which alternate on following rows.

MAKING A THREE-STITCH KNOT

Knots are always made on right-side rows.

1 Using the two-needle method and working into the front of the stitches only, cast on three stitches.

2 Knit the three cast-on stitches, then knit the original stitch again, making four new stitches on the right needle.

3 To complete the knot, lift three stitches, one at a time, over the last stitch on the right needle.

▶ The top row shows three-stitch knots, the bobbles on the other rows have five and seven stitches.

DIFFERENT YARNS WILL CREATE A VARIETY OF EFFECTS.

 TIP

The same bobble can look and behave differently depending on the number of turning rows.

MAKING A FIVE-STITCH BOBBLE

Bobbles are always started on a right-side row. This bobble is on reverse stockinette.

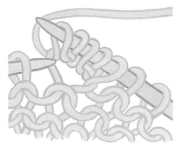 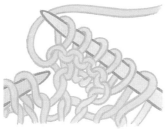

1 Into a stitch, work [k1, yarn over needle] twice, then k1 again, making five stitches on the right needle.

2 Then turn and purl the five stitches.

MAKING A SEVEN-STITCH LEAF

These three same-size leaves are each made slightly differently. But in all of them, paired increases are followed by pairs of decreases, worked at the sides or in the center.

▲ The leaf above has yarn-overs each side of the center stitch.

▲ Invisible lifted strand increases the shape of the base of this leaf.

▲ Seven stitches are worked into a double yarn-over at the start of this leaf.

3 To complete the bobble, turn, k5, turn, p2 together, p1, p2 together, turn, slip 2 knitwise, k1, pass the slipped stitches over. To vary this bobble don't decrease, lift the stitches over in the same way as the knot.

PARTY DRESS
Bobbles and leaves are a feature of this pretty outfit.

LEFT
This all-over nubbly pattern is also known as trinity stitch because three stitches are made from one and one from three on alternate rows.

1: BLACKBERRY STITCH

| ⍽ | [K1, P1, K1] ALL IN ONE ST |
| ⍽ | P3 TOG |

MULTIPLE OF 4 STITCHES

LEFT
Here, the very smallest possible knot adds texture to the smooth surface of a rib stitch worked through the back of the loop.

2: KNOTTED RIB

MULTIPLE OF 6 STITCHES PLUS 2

◎ K INTO FRONT, BACK AND FRONT OF ST MAKING 3 STS FROM ONE, LIFT 2ND AND FIRST STS OVER 3RD AND OFF NEEDLE.

3: 2 AND 3 BOBBLE RIB

MULTIPLE OF 5 STITCHES PLUS 2

◎ [K1, YO, K1,YO, K1] ALL INTO ONE ST MAKING 5 STS FROM ONE, TURN K5, TURN P5, LIFT 4TH, 3RD, 2ND AND FIRST STS OVER 5TH AND OFF NEEDLE.

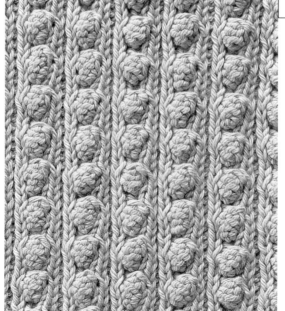

RIGHT
Crunchy bobbles are worked so closely together in this pattern that they make the rib spread out instead of pulling in.

RIGHT

Purl-stitch bobbles are placed in regular rows on stockinette stitch blocks, and outlined in alternating knit and purl stitches.

4: BOBBLE BLOCKS

MULTIPLE OF 6 STITCHES PLUS 1

5   *[K1, YO, K1, YO, K1] ALL INTO ONE ST, TURN K5, TURN, SKPO, K3 TOG, LIFT FIRST ST OVER 2ND AND OFF NEEDLE.*

5: BOBBLE AND WAVE

MULTIPLE OF 8 STITCHES

◎   *[K1, YO, K1, YO, K1] ALL INTO ONE ST, MAKING 5 STS FROM ONE, TURN K5, TURN P5, LIFT 4TH, 3RD, 2ND AND FIRST STS OVER 5TH AND OFF NEEDLE.*

ABOVE

The wave rib is not cabled, it's made with increases and decreases. The bobbles add an accent at the curve of each wave.

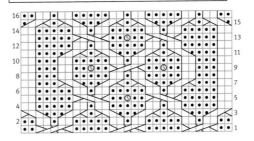

LEFT

This cable panel uses five-stitch cross, so there is a center stitch to place the bobble on.

6: BOBBLE AND BRAID CABLE

PANEL OF 29 STITCHES

◎   *[K1, YO, K1, YO, K1] ALL INTO ONE ST, MAKING 5 STS FROM ONE, TURN K5, TURN P5, LIFT 4TH, 3RD, 2ND AND FIRST STS OVER 5TH AND OFF NEEDLE.*

7: Triple Nosegay

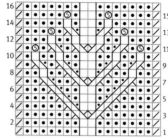

Multiple of 17 stitches plus 1

⊙ [K1, Y0, K1, Y0, K1] ALL
INTO ONE ST MAKING 5 STS
FROM ONE, TURN K5, TURN
P5, LIFT 4TH, 3RD, 2ND AND
FIRST STS OVER 5TH AND
OFF NEEDLE.

ABOVE
The traditional
nosegay pattern has
just two branches
with four bobbles.
Here the stitch
pattern has been
extended to three
branches and six
bobbles. Work
through the chart a
few times, and you
may see how to make
a nosegay pattern
with even more
branches.

RIGHT
Cabled ovals enclose
three crunchy, purl-
stitch bobbles. Again,
the large cable cross
uses five stitches to
give a center stitch to
place the bobbles on.

8: 3 Bobble cable

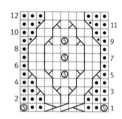

*Multiple of 10 stitches
plus 1*

⊙ AS ON TRIPLE NOSEGAY.

8: LARGE LEAF AND TWISTS

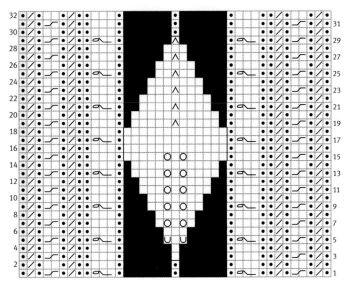

MULTIPLE OF 26 STITCHES PLUS 1

SL 1 PURLWISE, K1, YO, K1, LIFT SLIPPED ST OVER THE K1, YO AND K1 AND OFF NEEDLE.

ABOVE

The little twists at each side of the leaf are very simple, but as the leaf expands and contracts it curves the twists, making the pattern look more complicated than it really is.

10: STRAWBERRY BOBBLE

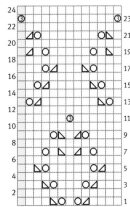

MULTIPLE OF 12 STITCHES PLUS 1

[K1, YO, K1] ALL INTO ONE ST MAKING 3 STS FROM ONE, TURN K3, TURN P3, LIFT 2ND AND FIRST STS OVER 3RD AND OFF NEEDLE.

LEFT

Bobbles can be used as an accent on lace stitches as well as cables. The berry motifs are arranged as a half-drop pattern here, but it would be easy to make a panel by repeating just the first 12 rows.

RIGHT
These pretty little
motifs have slender
leaves because the
open increases are
taken into the reverse
stocking stitch
background.

BELOW
The leaf framed in
the center of the
diamond is given a
separate chart to
make it easier to
follow the cable
pattern.

11: FLOWER SPRIGS

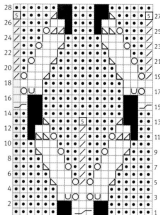

MULTIPLE OF 14 STITCHES PLUS 1

5 [K1, Y0, K1, Y0, K1] ALL INTO ONE ST MAKING 5
STS FROM ONE, TURN P5, TURN K5, LIFT 4TH, 3RD,
2ND ST, AND FIRST ST OVER 5TH AND OFF NEEDLE.

12: ORNATE CABLE WITH LEAF AND BOBBLES

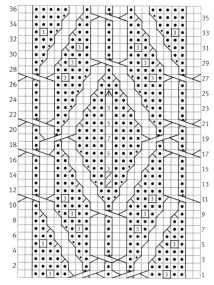

PANEL OF 25 STITCHES

WORK SUPPLEMENTARY LEAF
CHART EACH TIME THE 1
STITCH AND 11 ROW SYMBOL
IS INDICATED.

3 K INTO FRONT, BACK
AND FRONT OF ST
MAKING 3 STS FROM
ONE, TURN P3, TURN
K3, LIFT 2ND AND 1ST
ST OVER 3RD AND OFF
NEEDLE.

13: CELTIC VINE

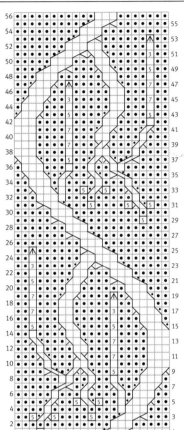

PANEL OF 21 STITCHES

5 *[K1, YO, K1, YO, K1] ALL INTO ONE ST, TURN P5 MAKING 5 STS FROM ONE, TURN K5, TURN P2 TOG, P1, P2 TOG, TURN S2KPO.*

WORK SUPPLEMENTARY LEAF CHART EACH TIME THE 1 STITCH AND 11 ROW SYMBOL IS INDICATED.

BELOW

The surface of this motif is only slightly raised because most of the increases have compensating decreases. The decrease taking five stitches into one at the top of each lobe takes a lot of words to describe but is easy to do if you remember that the stitches at each side are lifted alternately over the center stitch.

ABOVE

Inspired by Tree of Life carvings on early stone crosses, this design uses a separate small chart for the leaf to make it easier to follow the chart when working the curved, cabled stem.

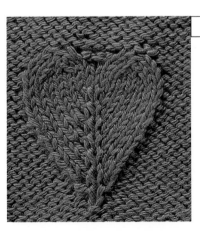

14: HEART LEAF

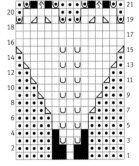

MOTIF OF 11 STITCHES, INCREASING TO 15 STITCHES

[SL 1 K] TWICE, [SL 1 P, LIFT 1 ST OVER AND OFF RIGHT NEEDLE, SL ST BACK ONTO LEFT NEEDLE, LIFT 1 ST OVER AND OFF LEFT NEEDLE] TWICE, P ST THAT REMAINS.

15: Afterthought flower

LEFT

This very adaptable motif is not quite an afterthought because you do need to plan enough moss stitch background and place the bobbles. You could vary the size and amount of the petals to suit the scale of your yarn.

16: Puff stitch

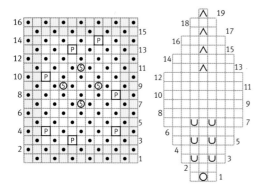

Multiple of 10 stitches plus 2

℘   *Lift strand between st but do not twist strand when knitting into it to make a small hole.*

9 stitches and 12 rows needed to place motif. A minimum of 7cm in moss stitch is needed all around this area to place the petals.

◎   *[K1, Y0, K1, Y0, K1] all into one st making 5 sts from one, turn P5, turn K5, lift 4th, 3rd, 2nd, and first sts over 5th and off needle.*

Work squares marked ℗ K on rs, p on ws for m-st, when you've finished knitting the background, lift the st indicated and work (K1, Y0, K1) into it for first row of supplementary petal chart. Continue working petal detached, then fasten off and sew in place.

ABOVE

Regular increases and decreases give a slightly raised surface to this pattern but it's easy to work because, despite making and losing stitches on each right side row, the stitch count remains constant.

17: WAVE AND KNOTS CABLE

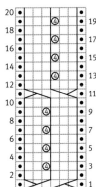

MULTIPLE OF 8 STITCHES

⊚   *K INTO FRONT AND BACK OF ST TWICE MAKING 4 STS FROM ONE, LIFT 3RD, 2ND, AND FIRST STS OVER 4TH AND OFF RIGHT NEEDLE.*

LEFT

Knots are faster to work than bobbles because you don't have to turn the work. You could substitute the large knot shown here with any of the smaller bobbles in other designs.

RIGHT

To work a frilled edging from this chart, cast on a multiple of 12 stitches plus four, then starting with the third row, k8 where the cast-on stitches are indicated. Follow the chart to make the bell shapes and you'll end with a stitch count that's a multiple of four.

18: BELL PATTERN

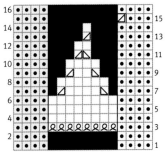

MULTIPLE OF 4 STITCHES PLUS 4

Ꝺ   *CAST ON ONE ST BY THE LOOP METHOD, TWISTING THE LOOP BEFORE PLACING IT ON THE NEEDLE.*

STRANDED COLOR KNITTING

All around the world, people have developed traditions of color knitting. Among the best known are patterns from Fair Isle, Scandinavia, Eastern Europe, and South America.

Most stranded color knitting is worked in stockinette with just two colors in a row. One or both of these colors may be changed on subsequent rows. Some patterns use three – or even four – colors in a row, but this can make the fabric very thick.

Stranded color knitting is usually worked from a chart. Reading the chart as directed, count the squares in the first color, and work that number of stitches. Then count and work the stitches in the second color. Continue counting and changing the colors along the row. Once you have established the first row, you can simply glance at the chart to see how the motifs change.

In many traditions, stranded color knitting is worked in the round, which means it's easy to see the pattern. If you're color knitting in the round, read each row of the chart from right to left. As you'll discover, most traditional Fair Isle patterns change color after no more than seven stitches in a row, with the yarn not in use stranded loosely on the wrong side of the work. Stranding across more stitches would make an over-long strand, so it's best if the yarn not in use can be woven in at regular intervals to keep the wrong side tidy.

USE LONG QUILTING PINS WHEN SEWING UP, SO THEY DON'T GET LOST IN THE KNITTING.

HOLDING THE YARNS

The simplest way to change colors is to drop one yarn and pick up the other. But for faster knitting, experiment with the following techniques.

HOLDING ONE YARN IN EACH HAND

Hold and work with one yarn in the right hand in the usual way. Tension the other yarn through the fingers of your left hand – or use the method on page 15. To knit with the left-hand yarn, insert the right needle, dip it under the yarn, and pull it through with a hook-like action. When purling, take care not to twist stitches.

HOLDING BOTH YARNS IN ONE HAND

Hold both the yarns in the right hand, with the main color over the first finger and the contrast color tensioned over the middle finger tip. Knit in the usual way with the main color, then turn the hand slightly to flick the yarn from the middle finger around the needle for the contrast stitches. On purl rows you may find it easier to manipulate the main color between thumb and first finger and the contrast over the first finger, still with the same rocking action of the wrist to take each yarn around the needle.

▼ STRANDING

The strands carried across should be tensioned loosely and evenly so that the knitting lies flat. Decide which color will lie on top and always strand the yarns in the same order.

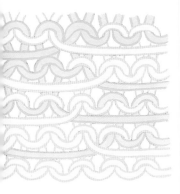

▼ WEAVING

The yarn not in use can be woven over and under on alternate stitches on the wrong side, making a very firm fabric. Or it can be woven in after several stitches. Take care the contrast color doesn't show through to the right side.

FAIR ISLE PATTERNS

▼ These little geometric patterns from Fair Isle, off the northern coast of Scotland, are called peerie patterns.

▶ This star motif is instantly recognizable as a Fair Isle pattern by the shaded effect.

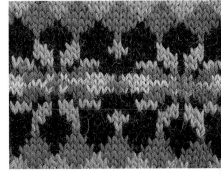

PATTERNED VESTS

Stranded color knitting makes distinctive vests, sweaters, and cardigans for all the family.

RIGHT

Little two and three row patterns like these are often used as a contrast between more complex bands of motifs. Have fun varying the colors on a striped background for an easy-to-knit version of classic Fair Isle.

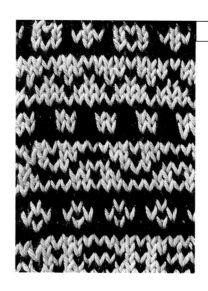

1: FAIR ISLE PEERIE PATTERNS

MULTIPLE OF 8 STITCHES PLUS 1

MULTIPLE OF 4 STITCHES PLUS 2

MULTIPLE OF 4 STITCHES PLUS 1

MULTIPLE OF 4 STITCHES PLUS 1

MULTIPLE OF 8 STITCHES PLUS 1

MULTIPLE OF 8 STITCHES PLUS 1

RIGHT

Some of these small borders are built up out of peerie patterns, while others stand alone. Here the background is all one shade; but for a more authentic color scheme, change the background for each band of pattern.

2: FAIR ISLE FLOWER BORDERS

MULTIPLE OF 20 STITCHES PLUS 1

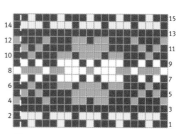

MULTIPLE OF 20 STITCHES PLUS 1

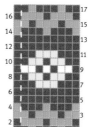

MULTIPLE OF 8 STITCHES PLUS 1

MULTIPLE OF 12 STITCHES PLUS 1

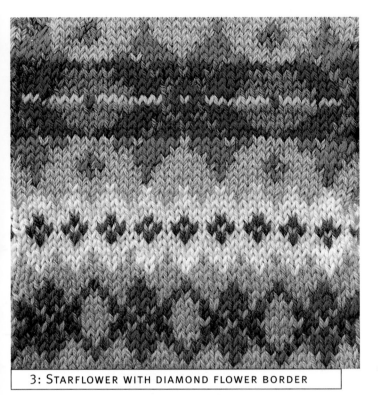

3: STARFLOWER WITH DIAMOND FLOWER BORDER

MULTIPLE OF 20 STITCHES PLUS 1

LEFT
Here, instead of shading gently, the color changes in the motif and the background are made on the same row, which adds to the jazzy feel of this bright interpretation of a traditional star with peerie patterns.

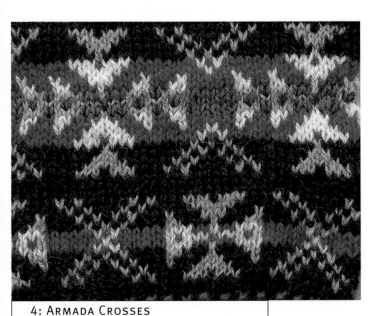

4: ARMADA CROSSES

MULTIPLE OF 24 STITCHES PLUS 1

LEFT
The first band of pattern shows a simple version of the cross; the second is more complex. Both of these are variations on X and O patterns. For an allover pattern, continue traveling the double line of yellow stitches over the navy background on rows 12, 13, and 14, then on rows 34, 35, and 36 to join up the X motifs.

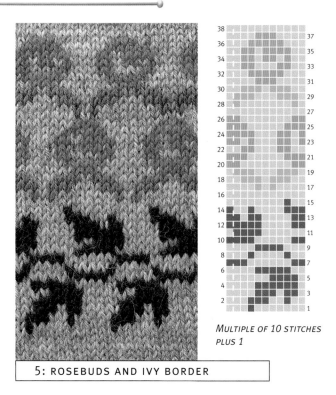

MULTIPLE OF 10 STITCHES
PLUS 1

5: ROSEBUDS AND IVY BORDER

6: HAREBELLS AND VINE BORDER

MULTIPLE OF 12 STITCHES
PLUS 1

ABOVE

These very pretty patterns are inspired by Swedish mittens. Work rows 17 to 26 for just one row of rosebuds, or repeat rows 17 to 38 for an allover pattern.

RIGHT

To space the rose motif as in the swatch, begin each subsequent repeat of the 9th row five stitches in from the right of the chart. Work the 10-row rose motif twelve times before the pattern repeats exactly on the 121st row.

7: ROSES AND VINE BORDER

MULTIPLE OF 12 STITCHES

ABOVE

The vine borders are shown running in opposite directions. If you want to knit the next band of harebells with the flowers facing right, read rows 9 to 31 in the opposite direction.

8: LITTLE STAR WITH SHADED WAVES

MULTIPLE OF 12 STITCHES PLUS 1

ABOVE

This little star shows how the tone of the colors you use can emphasize the motif. If you're choosing colors to work this motif, make sure that you substitute your darkest shade for the brown, moving through to the lightest shade for the warm white.

BELOW

Motifs similar to this South American geometric repeat can be found on pottery and basketwork, as well as knitting. Patterns like this are often used in the same way as peerie patterns in a Fair Isle.

9: SAWTOOTH BORDER

MULTIPLE OF 5 STITCHES PLUS 1

RIGHT

The large lightning pattern is based on an embroidery design. If you'd like to work a brighter version of this pattern, try working each zigzag and key motif in a different color. The smaller paddle and scroll motifs are similar to designs used in weaving.

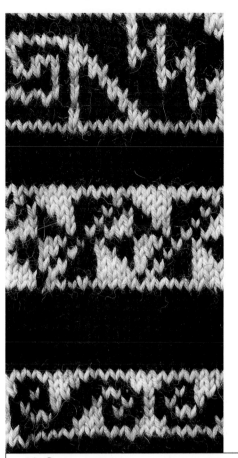

10: SOUTH AMERICAN GEOMETRIC PATTERNS

LIGHTNING

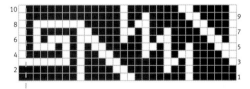

MULTIPLE OF 29 STITCHES PLUS 1

PADDLES

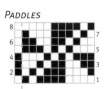

MULTIPLE OF 10 STITCHES PLUS 1

SCROLL

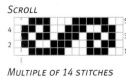

MULTIPLE OF 14 STITCHES PLUS 1

RIGHT

Worked in monochrome – black and white, or brown and natural, these versatile patterns are typically Scandinavian, but if you shade the background, they will look like Fair Isle. Similar patterns in solid, bright colors can be found on Turkish socks.

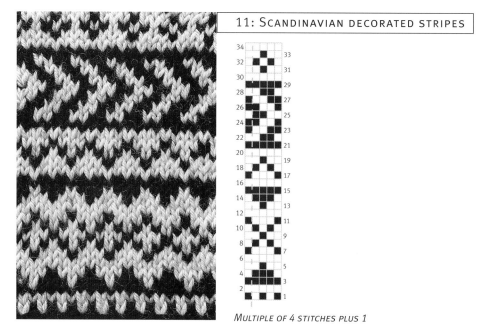

11: SCANDINAVIAN DECORATED STRIPES

MULTIPLE OF 4 STITCHES PLUS 1

RIGHT

The flea pattern at the top of this sample is one of those simple seeding patterns that can be varied with many different spacings, depending on the repeat of the pattern it's worked with. If you want to work the pretty Norwegian snowflake as an allover pattern, simply repeat rows 9 to 32.

12: SNOWFLAKE BORDER AND FLEA PATTERN

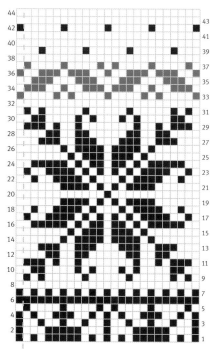

MULTIPLE OF 24 STITCHES PLUS 1

RIGHT

Although most of this
pattern has been
designed for stranded
knitting, you'll find it
easier to use separate
balls of black for the
reindeer body and in
for each area in red
between motifs.

13: LARGE REINDEER

MULTIPLE OF 30 STITCHES PLUS 1

RIGHT

You'll need to strand
three colors when
working this design:
pink, navy, and green.
Just loop the green
over a strand to carry
it across the large
gaps. The purple and
yellow petals are best
knitted with separate
lengths of yarn. This
design is very graphic
and would also work
well in two colors.

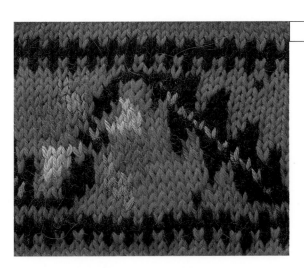

14: PERUVIAN FLOWER BORDER

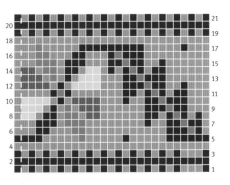

MULTIPLE OF 26 STITCHES PLUS 1

RIGHT
Strand the yarns for the purple background and pink leaf motifs, but use separate short lengths of contrasting color for each diagonal leaf vein. Change the contrasting color as often as you like.

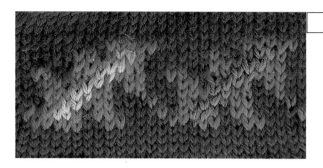

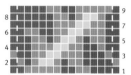

15: PERUVIAN LEAF BORDER

MULTIPLE OF 13 STITCHES PLUS 2

RIGHT
Use this simple geometric pattern to move from one area of solid color to another.

16: SOUTH AMERICAN WAVES

MULTIPLE OF 8 STITCHES PLUS 1

RIGHT
Little geometric border patterns contrasting with an allover design are typical of the patterns found on Latvian mittens. This design is quite easy to knit, as only row 22 has more than two colors.

17: LATVIAN STARS

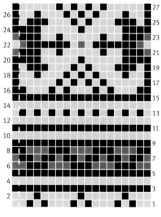

MULTIPLE OF 20 STITCHES PLUS 1

RIGHT

Use this striking star as a border or arrange it as a half-drop pattern.

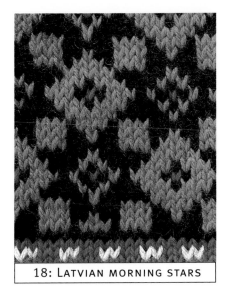

18: LATVIAN MORNING STARS

RIGHT

This simple pattern is easy to knit but capable of subtle variation. Try reversing the direction of the motif on a striped background.

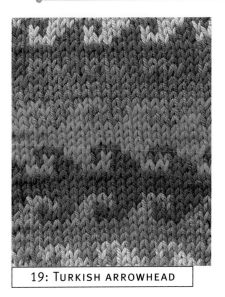

19: TURKISH ARROWHEAD

MULTIPLE OF 16 STITCHES PLUS 1

MULTIPLE OF 6 STITCHES PLUS 1

RIGHT

This allover pattern is a mirror image at each side of the center stitch. Here, the background color is changed every six rows, but you could use just one color or change the background as often as you wish.

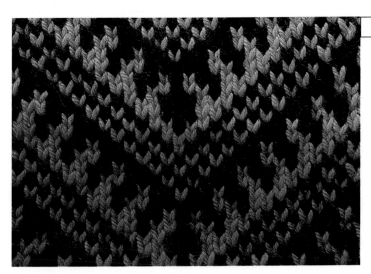

20: TURKISH SOCK PATTERN

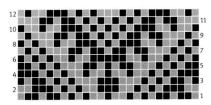

MULTIPLE OF 12 STITCHES
AT EACH SIDE OF CENTRE STITCH

INTARSIA COLOR KNITTING

Large geometric patterns, individual motifs, and picture knits are the kind of color designs that are best knitted using the intarsia technique.

Intarsia is simply working areas of color with separate balls of yarn which are linked together at each color change. This eliminates stranding or weaving in on the wrong side, and gives a single thickness fabric. The technique is used for flat knitting only – intarsia cannot be worked in the round.

Designs in intarsia are worked from charts where the number of stitches in each color can be seen clearly and easily. Stockinette is the most frequently used stitch, but the technique works just as well with textured stitches and cables.

Some designs – such as tiny blocks of color scattered on a plain background – are best worked in a combination of intarsia and stranding. Use separate lengths of yarn for small motifs, and strand the background color, twisting the yarns at each color change.

ORGANIZING THE YARNS

First sort out the yarns by counting the number of areas in each color, then wind off suitable lengths of yarn according to the size of the areas. Use complete balls of yarn for each large area. Wind the yarn on to bobbins for smaller areas or, if there are just a few contrast stitches, use a short length of yarn. If the design is very complex with lots of colors, avoid tangles by using lengths of yarn which can be pulled free easily because they are not attached to a ball or bobbin.

DIAGONAL COLOR CHANGES

It's easy to keep your knitting neat when working diagonals, because the colors move along one stitch each time. Linking the yarns at the changeover, therefore, comes naturally.

TIP

Reusable peel-off stickers are ideal for keeping your place in a chart. Position them above the row you're working from, so you can see how it relates to the pattern already knitted.

USE BOBBINS TO KNIT SMALL AREAS OF COLOR.

HOW TO LINK COLOR AREAS

Every time you change colors, you must link the areas together or there will be holes in your knitting. All you need to do is twist the yarns on the wrong side.

VERTICAL COLOR CHANGES

When the colors change at the same place on several rows, be particularly careful to twist the yarns neatly and evenly to avoid holes and loose stitches. Darn in ends along color changes.

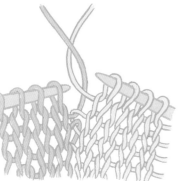

ON A KNIT ROW

Knit with the first color (here it's pink) to the changeover, then drop the yarn. Pick up the second color (purple) and take it around the first yarn before knitting the next stitch.

ON A PURL ROW

Purl with the second yarn to the changeover. Make sure you take the first yarn around the second yarn before knitting the next stitch.

KID'S SWEATER
Use the intarsia technique to create bold blocks of color or motifs like this world map.

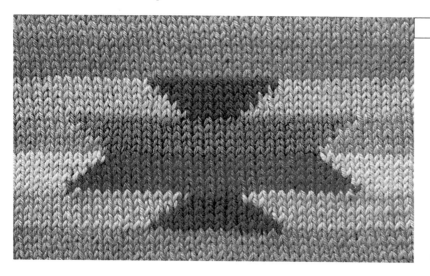

1: BROKEN STRIPES

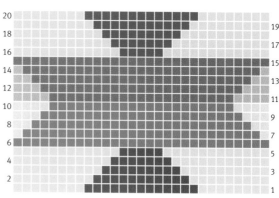

MOTIF OF 29 STITCHES

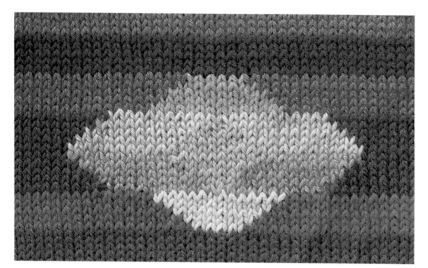

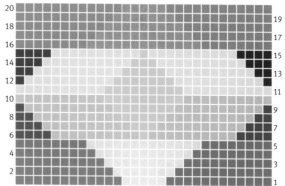

MOTIF OF 29 STITCHES

ABOVE AND TOP
One of the simplest exercises in intarsia is to use a few diagonal color changes to make motifs within stripes. Try light on dark or dark on light tonal variations.

RIGHT
By comparing the knitted design with the chart you can see how the drawing must be elongated to compensate for the fact that stockinette usually has more rows than stitches to a given measurement. In other words, to knit round spots you must chart ovals.

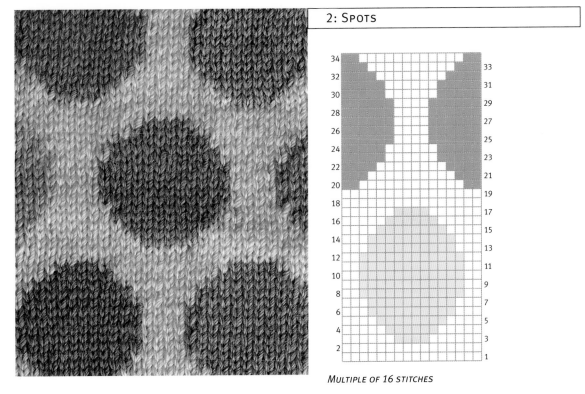

2: SPOTS

MULTIPLE OF 16 STITCHES

RIGHT
Even tiny patterns are better worked by the intarsia technique, so that there is no stranding behind the main background color.

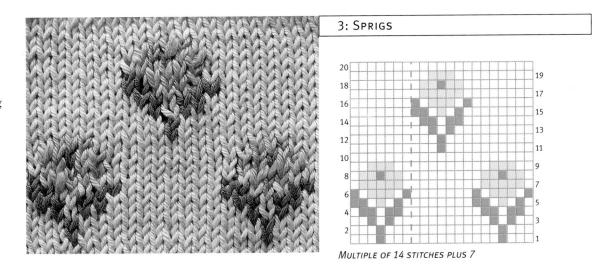

3: SPRIGS

MULTIPLE OF 14 STITCHES PLUS 7

RIGHT ABOVE AND BELOW

Checks and plaids, such as this pattern, are a classic way to use blocks of color. To keep the number of individual lengths of yarn to a minimum the overchecks can be worked in duplicate-stitch embroidery. The two designs share the same stitch count, but the diamonds (bottom right) are smaller, because the colors change on every row.

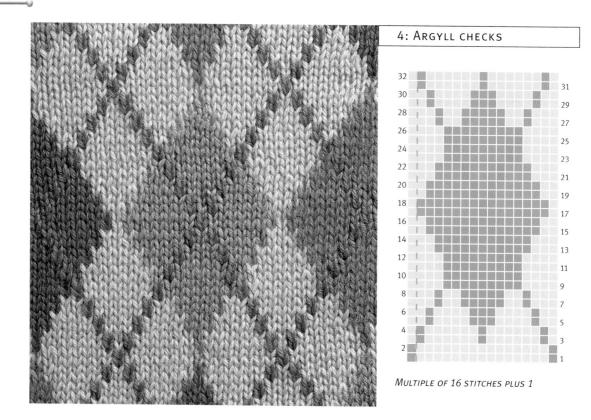

4: ARGYLL CHECKS

MULTIPLE OF 16 STITCHES PLUS 1

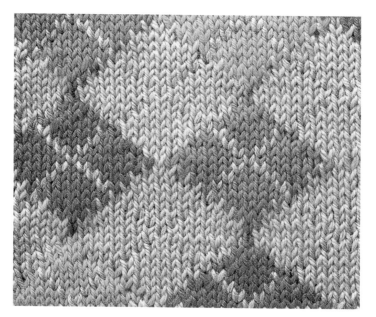

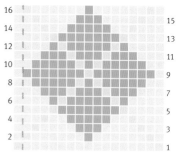

MULTIPLE OF 16 STITCHES PLUS 1

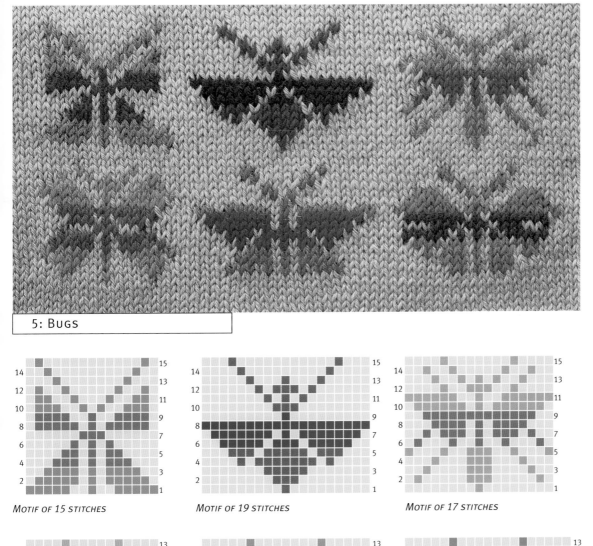

5: BUGS

LEFT
These stylized insects are made more lively with a central stripe of a deeper color. Use one or all of them as a repeat pattern or as individual motifs.

MOTIF OF 15 STITCHES

MOTIF OF 19 STITCHES

MOTIF OF 17 STITCHES

MOTIF OF 15 STITCHES

MOTIF OF 19 STITCHES

MOTIF OF 19 STITCHES

6: SOUTH AMERICAN BIRD

MOTIF OF 39 STITCHES

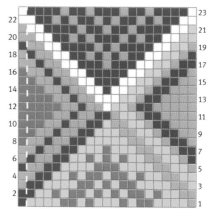

MULTIPLE OF 20 STITCHES PLUS 1

ABOVE

Based on a piece of Guatemalan weaving, this mixture of intarsia and stranded color knitting has a go-as-you-please border. The geometric repeat pattern avoids being too mechanical by having random color changes.

7: LEAVES

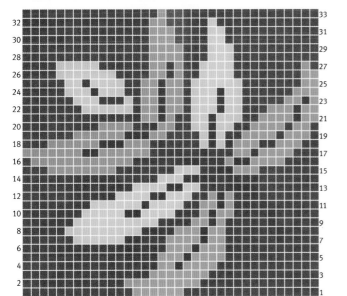

MOTIF OF 35 STITCHES

MOTIF OF 20 STITCHES

ABOVE
Almost any pictorial image can be knitted. The chart look taller than the motif because of the gauge.

RIGHT

This bright border design has a clear affinity with Fair Isle knitting, but instead of being the same color along the row, the daisies are each in a different color.

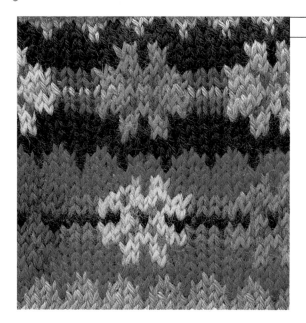

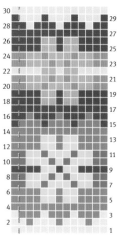

8: DAISY BORDER

MULTIPLE OF 12 STITCHES PLUS 1

RIGHT

Danish cross stitch was the inspiration for this crowned heart motif.

9: SCANDINAVIAN HEART

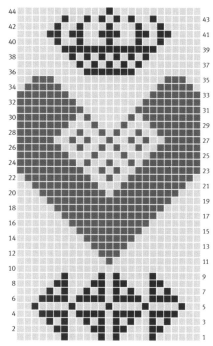

MOTIF OF 25 STITCHES

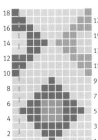

10: DIAMONDS

MULTIPLE OF 10 STITCHES PLUS 1

ABOVE

Simple geometric shapes are made more interesting by varying the colors. Instead of being carried along the row horizontally, the colors of the diamonds move diagonally up the design. The color of the square in the center of each diamond changes, and the background is a shaded, brushed mohair yarn.

11: FLOWER BORDER

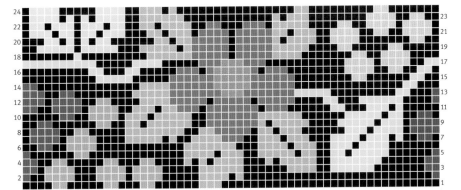

RIGHT

The flower head in this elaborate border design can be varied in color with each pattern repeat.

MULTIPLE OF 57 STITCHES

SPECIAL EFFECTS

When stitch pattern and construction technique become inextricably entwined, or when you add surface decoration to your knitting, you can create some very special effects.

Tucks and pleats can be used practically when designing a garment or creatively for sculptural pieces. Sometimes a stitch pattern takes over and becomes almost another way of knitting. Loops, for instance, are both on the surface and an integral part of the stitch. For a different approach to color knitting, try slip stitch patterns – some of these fascinating stitches are also reversible. Finally, there's no end to the ways you can add surface decoration to your knitting. Beads and sequins can be knitted in all over or placed dramatically. Embroidery can be planned to enhance a stitch pattern or to make marvelous motifs.

If you like working short rows and aren't afraid of picking up stitches, then you'll love entrelac. Using two colors and working in stockinette stitch makes it easy to understand the construction for your first attempt. But you can also work this woven-effect knitting in other stitch patterns, or you can add cables or color motifs to the blocks.

You'll need to re-think every stitch pattern for circular knitting. Whether you're creating flat or tubular shapes, the right side of the work is always facing you, making almost every kind of patterning easier to do.

▲ SEASHORE BEADS Even if they're large or irregular shapes, beads don't have to be sewn on afterwards – they can be knitted using the slip stitch technique.

▶ CROSS STITCH ROSE Cross stitch embroidery works beautifully on stockinette. Each cross stitch covers a single knitted stitch. However, as knitted stitches are wider than they are tall, the cross stitches won't be square. Take this into account when choosing or drawing a chart.

◄ MOTIF ENTRELAC These little boats look as though they're going up and down on the waves because of the different directions of the knitting. The opening and closing triangles are in contrast color. Each block of this entrelac is worked on 12 stitches and each boat motif is 9 stitches wide, leaving the edges clear for joining the blocks.

▼ SWEATERS IN THE ROUND Sweaters are so satisfying worked in the round, especially when combined with stranded color knitting. The body and sleeves are tubes shaped at the underarms, then the stitches are arranged – back, left sleeve, front, and right sleeve – to make one big round for the yoke. Plan the design so that the number of stitches in the first round divides exactly by the repeat of the pattern you have chosen. Decrease evenly in the rounds between the patterns to shape the yoke in at the neck.

◄ CIRCULAR SOCKS Traditional socks are simply tubes of knitting, worked on a set of double pointed needles. Start at the top and knit in rounds until you reach the heel. Work half the stitches of the next round with a contrast yarn, then work in a tube until you're ready to shape the toe. Undo the contrast yarn and shape the heel in the same way as you shaped the toe.

ENTRELAC

 The entrelac technique looks like magic, with the changing direction of the stitches making a woven fabric.

This technique uses short rows, decreases, and picked-up stitches, and the result is a patchwork that's actually knitted all in one. Each block has twice as many rows as stitches – the number of stitches used to make the base triangles determines the size of the blocks. You can use any stitch pattern you want, so long as the repeat or motif fits the number of stitches and rows for each block.

BASIC TECHNIQUE

The best way to understand the entrelac technique is to knit up a sample. This swatch of stockinette-stitch entrelacs is based on a multiple of 12 stitches. Use any yarn with appropriate-size needles, but change color for each row of blocks to emphasize the change in direction of knitting.

STARTING ROW OF BASE TRIANGLES

Using first color, cast on 36 sts. *1st base triangle* P2, turn, k2, turn, p3, turn, k3, turn. Purling one more stitch from left needle each time, continue in this way until there are 12 sts on right needle. Do not turn. Leave these stitches and work two more base triangles.

FIRST ROW OF BLOCKS

Change to second color. The first row of blocks has side triangles. *1st side triangle* K2, turn, p2, turn, kfb, skpo, turn, p3, turn, kfb, k1, skpo, turn p4, turn. Decreasing one stitch from base triangle on k rows each time, continue until kfb, k9, skpo has been worked, do not turn, leave these 12 sts. *Block* Pick up and k 12 sts from row-ends of base triangle, turn, p12, turn. K11, skpo, turn, p12. Continue in this way until all sts of base triangle have been decreased, do not turn. Work a second block between 2nd and 3rd base triangles. *2nd side triangle* Pick up and k 12 sts from row ends of last base triangle, turn, p2tog, p10, turn, k11, turn. P2tog, p9, turn, k10. Continue decreasing at beg of every purl row until one st remains, turn, slip st on to left needle.

SECOND ROW OF BLOCKS

Change to first color. The 2nd row of blocks does not have side triangles. *Block* P1, pick up and p 11 sts, turn, k12, turn. P11, p2tog, turn, k12. Continue in this way until all stitches of first row block have been decreased, do not turn. Work 2nd and 3rd blocks in this way.

COMPLETING THE ENTRELAC

The next row of blocks is the same as the first row of blocks but working into the 2nd row of blocks instead of base triangles. Alternating colors, work as many rows of blocks as you want, but always end with a first row of blocks, then finish off with triangles to give a straight edge at the top. *Closing triangles* Change to first color. P1, pick up and p 11 sts from row-ends of side triangle, turn, k12, turn. P2tog, p9, p2tog, turn, k11, turn. P2tog, p8, p2tog, turn, k10, turn. Continue in this way until turn, k2 has been worked, turn, p1, p2tog, turn, k2, turn, p3tog, 1 st remains. Picking up and purling 11 sts from row-ends of blocks, work 2nd and 3rd closing triangles.

ENTRELAC WITH CABLES

Adding a cable to your entrelac is fun. This swatch is based on a multiple of 12 stitches, but to balance the pattern, you'll need an extra edge stitch. Increase 1 st on the first row and decrease it on the last row of each block to work this six-stitch cable with 2 sts in reverse stockinette stitch on each side.

CIRCULAR KNITTING

Working in the round on double-pointed needles was probably the most common method of knitting until the end of the ninteenth century. Today, many knitters are rediscovering the advantages of this technique.

Because the right side of the work is always facing, it's actually easier to do almost every type of knitting in the round, including cables and especially stranded color patterns. For stockinette stitch, you just knit every round. Ribs and moss stitches are worked in the same way but on an even number of stitches. For garter stitch, you'll need to knit and purl alternate rounds.

Working from charts is simple: you just read each row of the chart from right to left, omitting any edge stitches. Cables can be crossed on any row, twist stitches can travel on every row, and color patterns are followed more easily. All kinds of seamless garments can be made in the round – hats, socks, gloves, and sweaters. Flat and round knitting can be combined to create garments that need the minimum of sewing up.

▶ This medallion is worked in six sections. The increase is a yarn-over made at the start of each section, giving a swirled effect.

KNITTING WITH DOUBLE-POINTED NEEDLES

Double-pointed needles can be bought in sets of four or five needles. Four is the minimum number of needles that can form a round – three needles to hold the stitches and one to knit with. But you can use as many double-pointed needles as you need for a larger project.

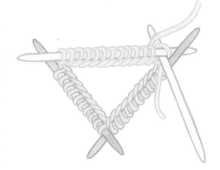

◀ Cast on in the usual way, dividing the number of stitches between all but one of the needles. Making sure that the stitches are not twisted on the needles, bring the first and last needles together and use the spare needle to knit with. At first it feels like all needles and not much knitting, but once you get the hang of organizing the needle tips, one end under and one over, you'll soon speed up. Take care to pull firmly on the yarn each time you work the first stitch on a new needle, or you could leave a ladder of loose stitches.

KNITTING WITH A CIRCULAR NEEDLE

Circular needles are perfect for knitting larger projects in the round. To start, simply cast on, then bring the needle ends together and knit. Before knitting the first round, make sure that the stitches are not twisted around the needle. Check again when you've worked the first round, or you could end up with a permanently twisted loop of knitting instead of a tube. Change to a smaller circular needle or a set of double-pointed needles if you decrease and the stitches no longer slide easily around the original needle.

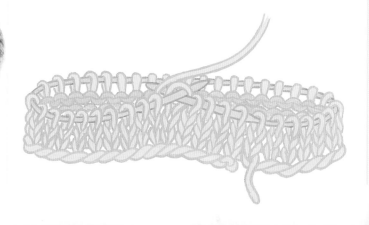

TUCKS AND PLEATS

Knitted fabrics needn't be flat. You can make three-dimensional effects like tucks and pleats without using a sewing needle.

TUCKS

Tucks are usually worked in stockinette stitch and are similar in construction to the hems on page 34. On the right side, fold your knitting along a row and knit each stitch on the needle together with the back loop of each corresponding stitch of a previous row. Stitches can be joined across the row to give a corded effect or to make a casing. You can use small groups of stitches to make bobbles. For a small bobble, turn, work five rows on three stitches, then join by knitting these stitches together with the three of the first row.

▲ The heavy tuck has a purl ridge along the fold, while the smaller tuck has a picot edge. The cord is only four rows deep and the bobbles are actually small tucks.

MOCK PLEATS

The curl of knit stitches rolling over purl stitches can be used to make a pleated fabric. Because they're based on rib, these stitch patterns make the fabric narrower and longer.

◄ To knit this kilted pleat effect, turn to page 52 and the Tree and Flags pattern. Cast on a multiple of eight stitches and repeat the stitches of one flag pattern only.

TRUE PLEATS

Plan your pleats in stockinette stitch and define the folds with slip stitches on right-side rows. Slip one stitch with the yarn in front for an inside fold; slip one stitch with the yarn at the back for an outside fold. At the top of the pleat, divide the stitches into three – for the face, turn-back, and underside. Slip these groups on to double-pointed needles and turn the needles to fold the fabric. Knit one stitch from each of the three needles together each time to close the top. Baste the pleats before pressing.

◄ This method can be used to make knife-edge pleats, box pleats, or inverted pleats.

LOOPS

Making an even, looped pile over the surface as you knit is a fascinating process. Much of the final effect depends on the type of yarn used and whether the loops are cut or uncut.

Loops are usually worked on alternate rows so that they all lie on the right side of the fabric. The density depends on whether the loops are made with one or more strands and whether they are worked on every stitch or on alternate stitches. Experiment with these two basic techniques to decide which suits your yarn.

▶ SINGLE LOOPS
Worked in cream wool and cut to give a sheepskin effect.

▶ DOUBLE LOOPS
Worked in a textured stretch yarn for a close pile surface.

SINGLE LOOP

This is a very secure loop that can be cut without unraveling. It's made on right-side rows of stockette stitch or garter stitch.

▲ Knit a stitch, but don't slip it off the needle. Bring the yarn to the front between the needles, take it clockwise around your left thumb and back between the needles. Knit the stitch on the left needle again and slip it off in the usual way.

▲ Insert the left needle into the fronts of the two new stitches on the right needle and knit them together through the back of the loops. When the knitting is finished the loops can be cut or they can be left uncut.

DOUBLE LOOP

Clusters of loops can be made on wrong-side rows of garter stitch. These clusters consist of two loops but you can make triple loops in the same way.

▶ Insert the needle in the next stitch as if to knit, but take the yarn over the right needle and first two fingers of the left hand twice, then over the needle again. Draw through, making three loops on the right needle, then insert the left needle and knit in the back and front of the loops to make two stitches on the right needle. Lift the first

stitch over the second and off the needle. This locks the loops fairly securely, but don't cut them.

SLIP STITCH COLOR KNITTING

If you want to create multi-colored knits but are worried about handling more than one color yarn at a time, then slip stitch color patterns are the answer. Only one color is used in a row.

These patterns are an easy way to create color effects – because the slip stitches are slipped to take the color over two rows. You don't need to strand colors along the row. For a reversible pattern, you'll sometimes need to work two consecutive rows in the same direction, so use a circular needle or double-pointed needles to make it easy to slide the stitches along to work from the other end.

SPOTTED STRIPES

◀ By slipping stitches and sliding at row ends you can achieve the effect of spots in the stripes. On the other side, the colors are reversed. After the first few rows, it's very easy to keep your place in this pattern.

Multiple of 4 sts plus 1. Circular needle. Colors A and B. Cast on with A, slide.
1st row Using B, p1, [k1, p1, sl1wyib, p1] to end, turn.
2nd row Using B, k1, [sl1wyif, k1, p1, k1] to end, slide.
3rd row Using A, k1, [p1, k1] to end, turn.
4th row Using A, p1, [k1, p1] to end, slide.
5th row Using B, p1, [k1, sl1wyif, k1, p1] to end, turn.
6th row Using B, k1, [p1, sl1wyib, p1, k1] to end, slide.
7th row Using A, as 3rd row, turn.
8th row Using A, as 4th row, slide.
These eight rows form the pattern.

GINGHAM CHECK

Multiple of 4 sts plus 2. Colors A, B, and C. Cast on with A
1st row (RS) Using A, k.
2nd row Using B, p2, [sl2wyif, p2] to end.
3rd row Using B, k2, [sl2wyib, k2] to end.
4th row Using A, p.
5th row Using C, sl2wyib, [k2, sl2wyib] to end.
6th row Using C, sl2wyif, [p2, sl2wyif] to end.
These six rows form the pattern.

▲Stitches are purled on all wrong-side rows, so this pretty check looks like stranded color knitting. When choosing your colors, for a true gingham effect, "A" should be the medium tone.

THE TROUSERS OF THIS CHARMING KNITTED MOUSE ARE WORKED IN GINGHAM CHECK.

BEADS AND SEQUINS

Knitting beads or sequins into the fabric gives some very exotic results. They can be worked all-over, in a regular pattern, or at random.

THREADING

The beads or sequins must be threaded on to the yarn before being knitted into the fabric. If possible, buy beads or sequins ready-strung, tie the fine nylon thread to the end of the knitting yarn, and slide them on to the yarn. Thread an estimated quantity, and when these are used up, break the yarn and thread a fresh quantity. Do this at the end of a row and darn in the ends in the usual way.

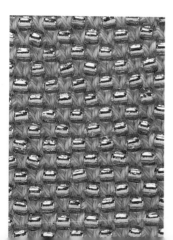

◀ To thread loose beads, take a piece of fuse wire about 2 in (5cm) long, lay the end of the knitting yarn across it, then bend it in half. Twist the two ends of fuse wire together and thread the beads.

◀ Working on alternate stitches and alternate rows gives this all-over effect. Slip several stitches to accommodate a large bead or bugle bead.

SLIPPING BEADS

The easiest way to knit with beads is the slip stitch technique, which can be used for almost any size of ornament. It's worked on the right-side of stockinette stitch.

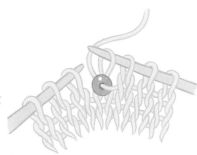

◀ Knit to the stitch where you want the bead, and bring the yarn to the front. Slide the bead along the yarn, and push it firmly up against the needle, as shown. Slip the stitch purlwise, take the yarn to the back, and knit the next stitch. This leaves the bead suspended in front of a stitch.

KNITTING SEQUINS

Sequins can also be worked by the slip stitch technique, but they lie better if they are worked into a stitch. This is done on the wrong side of stockinette stitch.

◀ Purl to the stitch where you want the sequin, insert the needle, take the yarn around in the usual way, then slide a sequin down to the needle. Complete the purl stitch, pushing the sequin through to the right side of the work. Secure the sequin on the next row by knitting into the back of the stitch

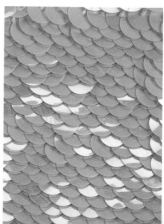

◀ Because of their flexibility, sequins can be pushed through a stitch more easily than beads. Closely worked beads or sequins can be used for bands and edgings as well as the whole fabric.

EMBROIDERY

Embroidery has a great affinity with hand knitting, you can use the same yarn, a contrast yarn, or an embroidery thread.

Plain stockinette can be used as a base or other stitch patterns can provide markers for positioning the embroidery. Use a tapestry needle and work between the strands of the knitting, rather than splitting the yarn. Because embroidery doubles the thickness of the fabric, it's better not used for large, solid areas.

DUPLICATE STITCH

Also called Swiss darning, this is a clever means of imitating multicolor knitting in stockinette.

1 Bring the needle out at the base of a stitch. Insert it from right to left under the two strands of the stitch above.

2 Take the needle into the base of the first stitch and out at the base of the next stitch. Continue making each duplicate stitch from right to left, covering knitted stitches.

CHAIN STITCH

Linear designs are very effective in chain stitch. Instead of working chain stitch with a tapestry needle, try using a medium-to-fine crochet hook – it's easier and faster. Chain stitch can also look very effective worked in the same yarn and color as the stockinette base.

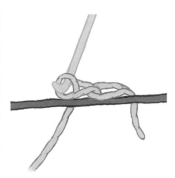

◀ Hold the thread underneath the work with your free hand and hold the crochet hook above. Take the hook down through the knitting and pull up a loop of yarn. Insert the hook in the next stitch and pull up a second loop through the first. Continue in this way working between knitted strands.

▶ These motifs were made freely with no guidelines. If you want to work a vertical line, perhaps up a rib, skip a strand occasionally to keep the chain lying flat.

EYELETS

Single and double eyelets in stockinette can be overcast with matching or contrasting stranded tapestry yarn. Work the eyelets at random or embellish a lace stitch pattern.

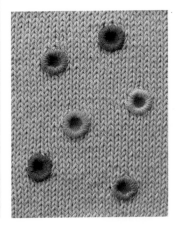

◀ Use a single strand of tapestry yarn to make a line of running stitches around the eyelet, then overcast the running stitches and the edge of the eyelet.

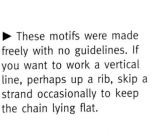

CHAPTER THREE

DESIGN
AND
INSPIRATION

HOW TO DESIGN

Inventing a design is simply a matter of common sense, a few calculations – and your imagination!

There are probably as many different ways of working out a set of instructions as there are designers, but here's some advice to get you started. First, you need a source of inspiration. The idea for a design may be inspired by the texture of a yarn, an exciting range of colors, a fashion trend, a combination of stitch patterns, a motif, or a construction technique. Next, choose your yarn, experiment with stitch patterns, and knit up some swatches. When you're happy with the look and feel of the swatch, reach for the tape measure and the calculator, and begin to plan your sweater.

Measuring

You'll need two sets of measurements to work out your design.

First, write down the gauge of your swatch as so-many stitches and so-many rows to 4 inches (10 cm). This will be more accurate than measuring a smaller unit such as 1 inch (1 cm). Do the same for the row gauges.

Second, plan the size and shape of each piece you're going to knit. The easiest way to be sure that you'll get the fit you want is to measure an existing garment. Alternatively, you can take your body measurements and add movement room to suit the style of your design.

TIP

Experiment first with a natural-fiber yarn. Then, if you need to unravel a section of your knitting, you can simply steam out the crinkles by holding the yarn over a recently boiled kettle, and re-use the yarn. Rewind it very loosely.

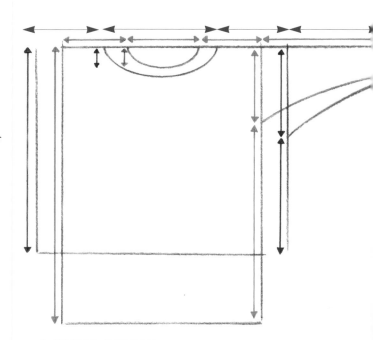

▲ A SIMPLE SWEATER

These two variations on a simple drop-sleeve sweater show how different proportions can be used to create two sweaters measuring the same from cuff to cuff.

Using the diagram above as a guide, fill in your measurements. All knitting measurements should be taken with the tape measure held straight along rows or stitches – never take it around curves or along shaped edges.

The diagram shows only half of the sleeve, so the top edge and cuff edge measurements must be doubled when calculating the width of the sleeve. For a fitted style or a shaped armhole, you'll need to take more measurements.

It's a good idea to decide on the proportions of your design by making a scale drawing on graph paper, allowing one square for each inch or centimeter. This is useful if you are calculating the shape of a sleeve top in relation to the depth of an armhole, since the number of stitches and rows in the corresponding edges may vary and must be calculated separately.

If you are working out unfamiliar shapings, you could make a full-size paper pattern before you think about stitches and rows.

Number crunching

To translate your measurements into stitches and rows, use a calculator for speed and accuracy. Here, measurements are given in inches and centimeters, but always work in one or the other – don't mix them. For example, if your gauge is 22 stitches to four inches (10 cm), divide the stitches by 4 (10) to give 5.5 stitches per inch (2.2 stitches per cm).

How many stitches to cast on for a width of 24 inches with a gauge of 5.5 stitches to one inch?
5.5 multiplied by 24 = 132 stitches

How many stitches to cast on for a width of 61 centimeters with a gauge of 2.2 stitches to one centimeter?
2.2 multiplied by 61 = 134 stitches

Calculate the number of rows to a given measurement in the same way, using the row gauge.

Planning repeats

If you're using stockinette stitch, you can cast on the precise number of stitches needed for the width (plus two stitches which will be lost in the side seams when they are sewn up). Add or subtract a stitch or two to balance a ribbed edge. If you're using a textured stitch pattern, you will have to calculate how many multiples of the pattern – plus any edge stitches – come closest to fitting into your measurements. Check the row repeats in relation to the length in the same way.

Stockinette can be worked on any number of rows, but if working in a textured stitch, you may want to shape the shoulder or neck at the end of a pattern repeat, or on a specific pattern row to avoid an ugly break. Change measurements or adapt stitch patterns until you are happy with the proportions of your design.

▼ **PLAN YOUR GARMENT**
Before you measure up and plan a garment, make sure you have diagrams, swatches, and samples of yarn to hand.

PLAYING WITH COLOR

INTARSIA MOTIFS

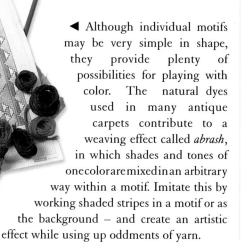

Chart motifs individually
before planning the design.

▲ Because kelim motifs are
quite large, they specifically
lend themselves to intarsia
multi-color knitting (see pages
114 – 123), which means that
you only have to establish a
stockinette-stitch gauge in
the yarn you want to use in
order to estimate the size of
your design.

▲ Kelims and old woven
textiles are a rich source of
ideas for color and pattern.
The designs are geometric,
which makes them easy to
interpret on a chart.

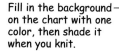

Fill in the background
on the chart with one
color, then shade it
when you knit.

◀ Although individual motifs
may be very simple in shape,
they provide plenty of
possibilities for playing with
color. The natural dyes
used in many antique
carpets contribute to a
weaving effect called *abrash*,
in which shades and tones of
one color are mixed in an arbitrary
way within a motif. Imitate this by
working shaded stripes in a motif or as
the background — and create an artistic
effect while using up oddments of yarn.

SMALL REPEAT PATTERNS

If you love multi-color knitting, you'll find inspiration wherever you look. This little Buddha figure, with its patterned and plain areas, sparks off lots of color combinations for these swatches. When you choose colors, don't worry too much about matching them exactly to your inspiration. A color may look too bright in the ball, but used in tiny amounts it will wake up the softer shades. Mix in a few yarns with a slight texture to break up the regularity of the surface. Start by using the classic "two colors in a row" stranded knitting technique (see pages 104 – 105), then add more colors or incorporate tiny areas of intarsia. Or simply start to knit and change the colors whenever you like.

Color more than one repeat to see the effect of the pattern.

▶ Use a chart with a small repeat, such as the Fair Isle peerie patterns, and try out the effect of changing the background color and the pattern color each time to give a flickering, striped effect. The motifs don't need to be very complicated, as even the simplest little patterns come to life if you get the colors right.

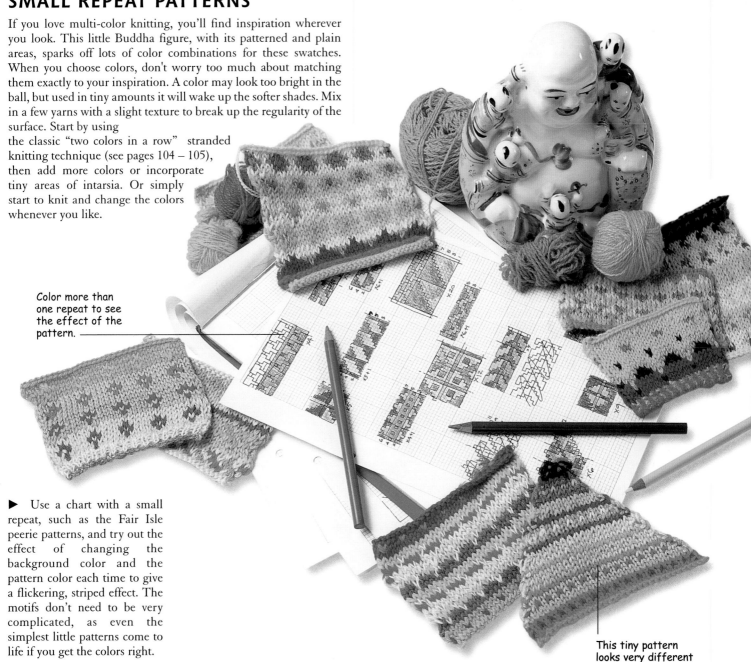

This tiny pattern looks very different as the colors change.

ADAPTING A CROSS STITCH CHART

Keen color knitters are often tempted to knit from cross stitch charts. If you do, remember that each cross stitch on fabric is square, whereas each knitted stitch is a wide and short V shape. With the stranded knitting technique, you may have an almost square gauge which doesn't distort the design too much. But if you use the intarsia technique to knit directly from a cross stitch chart, the design will be compressed vertically.

▲ For a picture knit or a motif to be instantly recognizable – such as these letters inspired by old cross stitch samplers – you'll need to design a chart with the proportions of the gauge in mind.

◄ The easiest way to design a chart is to work out exactly the number of stitches and rows that the motif will need in your gauge on graph paper, then fill in the design.

Light letters on a dark background emphasize the typographical effect.

DESIGNING A MOTIF

▲ Charting a flower pattern is a fascinating project to take on. Choose something that's easily recognizable, such as a pansy.

▲ Draw the flowers as accurately as you can given the limitations of the graph paper, which make true curves difficult. Small motifs can be worked in stranded knitting.

◀ Larger motifs or posies of flowers are best if the small areas of a particular color are intarsia-knitted and the background is stranded. Test the technique and the way the design looks by knitting swatches until you get the desired effect. When you've designed the motif, draw a full-size chart for the back of the garment, photocopy your motif several times, then cut out the motifs and move them around on the large chart until you desired effect.

Try designing subtle variations instead of working identical flowers.

PLACING A MOTIF ON A SIMPLE SWEATER

▼ If you're knitting a complex motif, it's best to keep the shape of the sweater simple. To establish your gauge, knit a swatch from part of the chart, then work out the size of the motif. Although you can add more background or frame the motif with another pattern, the size of the motif will dictate the proportions of your sweater.

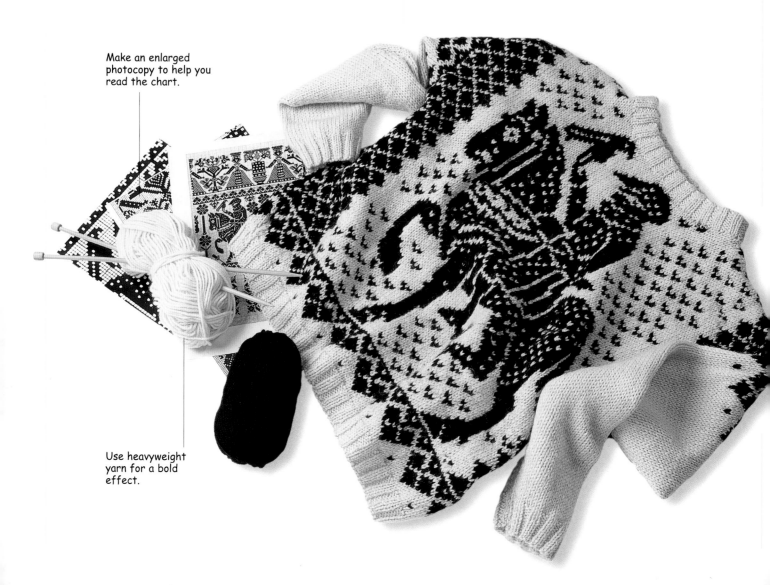

Make an enlarged photocopy to help you read the chart.

Use heavyweight yarn for a bold effect.

DESIGNING A CARDIGAN

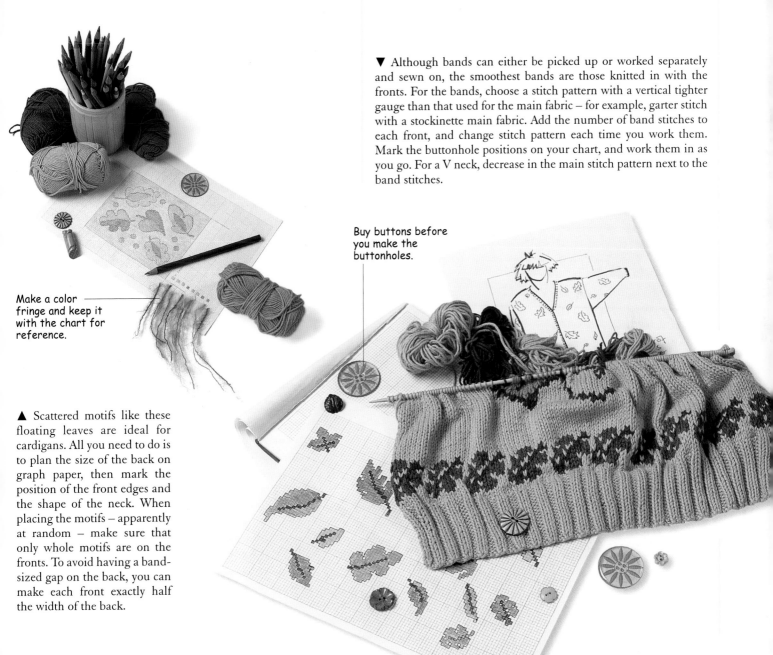

▼ Although bands can either be picked up or worked separately and sewn on, the smoothest bands are those knitted in with the fronts. For the bands, choose a stitch pattern with a vertical tighter gauge than that used for the main fabric – for example, garter stitch with a stockinette main fabric. Add the number of band stitches to each front, and change stitch pattern each time you work them. Mark the buttonhole positions on your chart, and work them in as you go. For a V neck, decrease in the main stitch pattern next to the band stitches.

Buy buttons before you make the buttonholes.

Make a color fringe and keep it with the chart for reference.

▲ Scattered motifs like these floating leaves are ideal for cardigans. All you need to do is to plan the size of the back on graph paper, then mark the position of the front edges and the shape of the neck. When placing the motifs – apparently at random – make sure that only whole motifs are on the fronts. To avoid having a band-sized gap on the back, you can make each front exactly half the width of the back.

COMBINING CABLES AND COLOR

▼ Creating a design with cable stitches is just like planning any other repeat pattern – all you have to do is use the gauge to work out the measurements. The only difference is that if you are combining cables with another stitch pattern, or putting different cables together, you'll need to take the gauge of each cable panel and stitch pattern separately. Calculate the size of each panel, then add them together to establish the width. To adjust the design to get the measurement you want, change the number of stitches between panels.

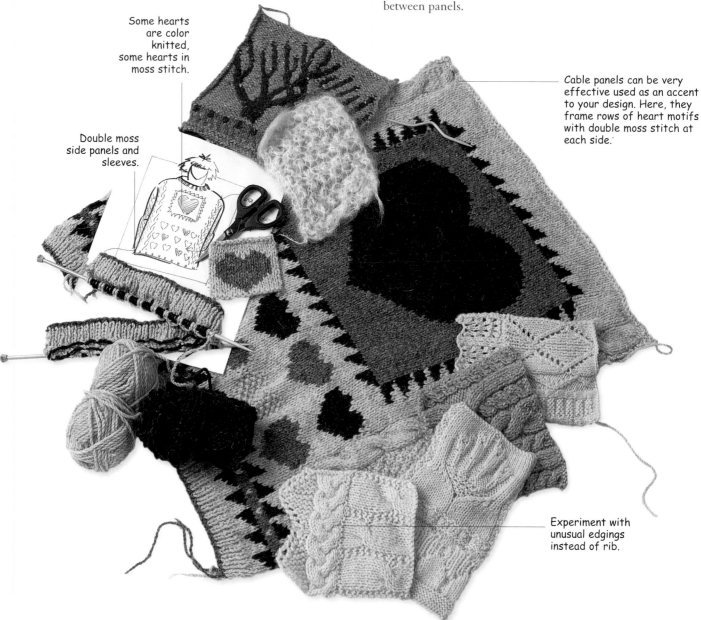

Some hearts are color knitted, some hearts in moss stitch.

Double moss side panels and sleeves.

Cable panels can be very effective used as an accent to your design. Here, they frame rows of heart motifs with double moss stitch at each side.

Experiment with unusual edgings instead of rib.

DESIGNING A CIRCULAR YOKE

▼ Traditional techniques don't have to be worked in traditional colors. Here, an unusual random-dyed yarn breaks up the very simple stranded color pattern, making it appear more complicated.

◄ For this circular yoke design, the back, front, and sleeves are worked flat. When they're joined in a round, each band of pattern will different, to create a rich effect and to fit in with the changing stitch counts as the yoke is decreased.

Circular yoke with decreases between the bands of pattern.

◄ There are two ways to plan a circular yoke. With narrow bands of pattern, think of the decrease rounds as concentric circles closing in toward the center and place the decreases in the unpatterned background between the bands. For large motifs, imagine the yoke with wedge-shaped segments and decrease between the motifs. Space the decreases far apart at the start, then work fewer rounds between decreases to bring the yoke in as you get up to the neck.

All edges have a rolled finish.

GALLERY

You can knit a work of art to hang on the wall, but you're more likely to make something to wear, just as knitters have done for generations. Here you can see a selection of vintage designs, then turn the pages for a look at the best in contemporary knitting.

Nostalgia

This collection of old knitting patterns is an insight into the fashions of yesterday.

1920s

The comfort and elasticity of knitted fabric has made it popular for baby clothes for at least a century. Knitting magazines, such as this one on the left, contain interesting early baby knits, including items such as body belts and gaiters.

In the early part of the twentieth century, little boys wore skirts and looked remarkably like little girls. But as they grew up, in spite of keeping their curls, they wore more boyish clothing, like this two-piece suit, bottom left.

The movement away from structured, corseted fashions brought knitwear to the fore. This long lace-stitch sweater, right, worn with a cloche hat, is typical of the 1920s.

As sporting activities became popular leisure pursuits, more knitting was worn. Fair Isle sweaters began to be worn by golfers and non-golfers alike, see right. Cycling, skating, hiking, and, in England, cricket all generated knitted fashions.

1930s

Folk traditions began to be adapted for fashion and everyday wear. One such strong influence was the Tyrolean look, which was popular for at least a decade.

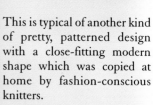

This is typical of another kind of pretty, patterned design with a close-fitting modern shape which was copied at home by fashion-conscious knitters.

1940s

During two world wars, knitted garments were a must for servicemen and women. After the Second World War – in spite of great austerity – fashion was extreme to the point of exaggeration. Shoulders were heavily padded to give a clear-cut silhouette and knitting was no exception. Anyone who could knit could produce the latest look.

There was less choice in ready-made clothes in the 1940s and people economized by hand-knitting garments that we wouldn't dream of making today, including coats, dresses, hats, stockings, underwear, and swimsuits.

1950s

By the middle of the twentieth century, fashion became more light-hearted and informal. A craze for chunky pictorial sweaters and jackets swept across the United States and Britain.

At about the same time, the "Sloppy Joe" sweater was worn in places ranging from the United States to the left bank in Paris, France.

1960s

As the 1960s progressed, hand-knitting lent itself to all kinds of fashions, from mini skirts to hot pants. Since then, knitting has established a sense of identity based on its own traditions, rather than merely imitating other trends.

Aran cabled knitting had a revival of popularity and spread to catwalks and stores across the world. Here Aran is shown looking fashionable, rather than homespun.

CONTEMPORARY DESIGN

Fresh and full of vitality, knitting today is an eclectic mix of traditional techniques and modern style.

Kaffe Fassett

Kaffe's distinctive approach to hand knitting has persuaded knitters everywhere to be more adventurous. His timeless ideas – inspired by ethnic and decorative arts – are wonderful examples of color knitting.

▲ **CHATTERBOX**
Here, a multitude of bright and rich colors flicker across a whirl of tiny triangles.

▲**PINWHEEL**
Eighteen colors are brilliantly combined in this exciting geometric design.

▲ STONE CIRCLES

This design shows a free interpretation of organic shapes with monochromatic shading.

◄ CHINA CLOUDS

Subtle differences in the patterning and strong colors add variety to this very bold design.

► ROSE PETALS

Ovals of color seem to float on a neutral background for this neat little jacket.

COLOR

From couture to classics, flamboyant or restrained, color is an essential element in these contemporary designs.

▲ **JEAN MOSS**
PEARMAIN SWEATER: Here, color motifs are delicately combined with textured stitches and cables.

▲ **LOUISA HARDING**
LIMERICK: Traditional Fair Isle is given a modern interpretation in this classic sweater.

► **JEAN MOSS**
HAUSA JACKET: This boldly colored design is inspired by African textiles.

▲ **JULIEN MACDONALD**
CATWALK: Anarchic student catwalk fashion gives chunky knitting a bold look.

▲ KIM HARGREAVES

LAUREL LEAF: Pretty leaf shapes in soft colors drift across this little cardigan.

◀ SANDY BLACK

SHAWL CARDIGAN: Real tassels add to the trompe l'oeil effect of this design.

▲ MARTIN STOREY

BANNER JACKET: Bold stars and stripes are worked in intarsia for this striking design.

◀ VIVIENNE WESTWOOD

CATWALK: The unusual combination of a nubbly, multicolored yarn and scaled-up Shetland lace gives this design great impact.

STITCH

Richly textured cables and bold shapes, or simple stitches and exquisite tailoring are the design ingredients for these contemporary classics.

▲ ALICE STARMORE
ST. BRIGID: Celtic knotwork cables are used to dramatic effect in this fringed sweater.

▲ ALICE STARMORE
ST. CIARAN: Soft, heather yarn is used for this generous shawl with wide Celtic cable panels.

▲ KIM HARGREAVES
PALM: Edge-to-edge styling in moss stitch makes this design cool and sophisticated.

◄ KIM HARGREAVES
PUNCH: Bold bands of color add emphasis to simple stitches and a tailored shape.

KNITTING FOR KIDS

Style and fashion sense start early with these designer hand knits and toys.

◄ KATIE MAWSON
HEN AND FISH SWEATERS: Farmyard and seaside themes give a picture-book feel to these colorful designs.

▲ DEBBIE BLISS
SMALL RABBIT WITH SWEATER: Debbie is well known for her children's knitwear, but she also designs original toys like this cute rabbit.

▲ JEAN MOSS
POOKA: Color patterned borders and a mixture of cables and garter stitch are used to make this bright, button-neck sweater.

◄ ALICE STARMORE
ELEPHANTS: Silhouette motifs are shaded in Fair Isle style for this little vest.

KNITTING FOR FUN

A sense of humor and a wild imagination

characterize these works of art.

◄ **SANDY BLACK**
◄ SANDY BLACK
LEOPARD AND CAT: These fun scarves are knitted in soft, brushed yarns.

▲ **FREDDIE ROBINS**
TREE COSIES: These witty knits are a verbal pun and visual joke.

▲ **LEO**
KNITTED TROPHIES: Is it a sock or is it a glove? No, it's art inspired by childhood memories of shadow puppets.

WORLDWIDE COLOR

Past and present combine in these recent examples of Peruvian and Turkish traditional hand knitting.

▲ EASTERN TURKEY
GLOVES: Simply shaped to fit either hand, these gloves are patterned front and back with tassels on the fingertips.

▲ SOUTH AMERICA
PERUVIAN MARKETPLACE: These knitted hats are a wonderful line-up of color and pattern.

▲ EASTERN TURKEY
SLIPPERS: The motifs on these modern slippers are inspired by traditional socks and interpreted in bright synthetic yarns.

▲ EASTERN TURKEY
SOCKS: These cream and black woollen socks are traditional in stitch and pattern.

▶ SOUTH AMERICA
PERUVIAN HATS: Fine yarn is knitted in the round on hooked needles to make these intricately patterned hats.

READING CHARTS

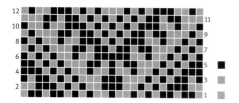

Each square of the chart represents a stitch and each row of squares represents a row of stitches.

The numbers up the sides of the chart are row numbers and you need to progress from the bottom to the top of the chart, like knitting itself.

All rows that are numbered on the right-hand side of the chart are read from that side and represent right-side rows. All rows that are numbered on the left-hand side of the chart are read from that side and represent wrong-side rows.

Black squares or black areas on charts are not included in a stitch count. They are used where stitches do not exist (for example, where a stitch is lost by decreasing and is not compensated for with an increase).

Shaded areas show edge stitches or extra stitches used to balance patterns. Unshaded areas show a panel or the multiple of stitches to repeat. The number of stitches in a panel or multiple is given underneath the chart, plus the extra stitches (for example, a multiple of 8 sts plus 2 means multiply 8 by the number of repeats required and then add the 2 end stitches to balance the pattern).

Sometimes stitches are outlined to make reading the chart easier – this doesn't affect how the stitches are worked.

KEY TO CHART SYMBOLS

	k on RS rows, p on WS rows
	p on RS rows, k on WS rows
	k1tbl on RS rows, p1tbl on WS rows
	no stitch
	sl1wyif on RS rows, sl1wyib on WS rows
	sl2wyif on RS rows, sl2wyib on WS rows
	sl5wyib on WS rows
	sl1wyib on RS rows, sl1wyif on WS rows
	k in front and back of stitch
	lift strand between stitches and k into back of it
	lift strand between stitches and p into back of it
	yarn forward and over needle to make a stitch
	k2 together
	p2 together
	sl1 knitwise, k1, pass slipped st over
	sl1 knitwise, k2tog, pass slipped st over
	sl2sts as if to work k2tog, k1, pass slipped sts over
	sl1 st on to cable needle and hold at back; k1, then k1 from cable needle
	sl1 st on to cable needle and hold at front; k1, then k1 from cable needle
	on either RS or WS rows, sl1 st on to cable needle and hold at back; p1, then k1 from cable
	on either RS or WS rows, sl1 st on to cable needle and hold at front; p1, then k1 from cable needle
	sl2 sts on to cable needle and hold at back; k1, then p2 from cable needle
	sl1 st on to cable needle and hold at front; p2, then k1 from cable needle
	sl1 st on to cable needle and hold at back; k2, then p1 from cable needle

	sl1 st on to cable needle and hold at front; p1, then k2 from cable needle
	sl2 sts on to cable needle and hold at back; k2, then k2 from cable needle
	sl2 sts on to cable needle and hold at front; k2, then k2 from cable needle
	sl2 sts on to cable needle and hold at back; k2, then p2 from cable needle
	sl2 sts on to cable needle and hold at front; p2, then k2 from cable needle
	sl1 st on to cable needle and hold at back; k3, then p1 from cable needle
	sl3 sts on to cable needle and hold at front; p1, then k3 from cable needle
	sl3 sts on to cable needle and hold at back; k2, sl1 st from cable needle on to left needle and p this st, k2 from cable needle
	sl3 sts on to cable needle and hold at back; k2, sl1 st from cable needle on to left needle and k this st, k2 from cable needle
	sl2 sts on to cable needle and hold at back; k3, then p2 from cable needle
	sl3 sts on to cable needle and hold at front; p2, then k3 from cable needle
	sl3 sts on to cable needle and hold at back; k3, then k3 from cable needle
	sl3 sts on to cable needle and hold at front; k3, then k3 from cable needle
	k into front of 2nd st, k into back of 1st st, sl both sts off left needle together
	k into front of 2nd st, p into front of 1st st, sl both sts off left needle together
	k into back of 2nd st, k into front of 1st st, sl both sts off left needle together
	p into back of 2nd st, k into front of 1st st, sl both sts off left needle together
	k into front of 3rd st, then 2nd st, then 1st st, sl3 sts off left needle together
	k into front of 3rd st, p into front of 1st st, then 2nd st, sl3 sts off needle together
	p into back of 3rd st, then 2nd st, k into front of 1st st, sl3 sts off left needle together

NEEDLE SIZES

Metric	American	old UK sizes
2	0	14
2 1/4	1	13
2 1/2	-	-
2 3/4	2	12
3	-	11
3 1/4	3	10
3 1/2	4	-
3 3/4	5	9
4	6	8
4 1/2	7	7
5	8	6
5 1/2	9	5
6	10	4
6 1/2	10 1/2	3
7	-	2
7 1/2	-	1
8	11	0
9	13	00
10	15	000

ABBREVIATIONS

- c3bp – on WS rows, sl2 sts on to cable needle and hold at back, k1, then p2 from cable needle
- c3fp – on WS rows, sl1 st on to cable needle and hold at front, p2, then k1 from cable needle
- k – knit
- p – purl
- rem – remaining
- RS – right side
- skpo – sl1 knitwise, k1, pass slipped st over
- s2kpo – sl2 sts as if to work k2tog, k1, pass slipped st over
- sl – slip
- ssk – sl 1st st, then 2nd st, knitwise, insert left needle into sts and k2tog
- st(s) – stitches
- tbl – through back of loop
- tog – together
- wyib – with yarn in back
- wyif – with yarn in front
- WS – wrong side
- yfwd – yarn forward
- yo – yarn over needle
- * – st left on needle
- [ ] – work instructions in brackets as directed

GLOSSARY

Aran - sweater design with cables, bobbles, and textured stitch patterns in natural, cream wool; originally associated with the Aran Islands, Ireland, it can now mean a design with cable patterns

Argyll - Scottish tartan sock pattern, now used to describe a diamond pattern with a superimposed plaid

back (of work) - the side of the work away from the knitter

bobbin - (i) shape for winding on lengths of yarn; used for multi-color knitting (ii) wooden tube with four pegs at top, used for 4-stitch tubular knitting

brushed - yarn with surface hairs raised in the manufacturing process

casting on - making stitches on needle at start of work

casting off (binding off) - closing stitches at end of work

chart - (i) grid with colors or symbols representing motifs or stitch patterns (ii) complete garment shape marked out on graph paper

crossed stitches - stitches worked through the back of the loop

eyelets - holes made with yarn-overs and decreases; part of a lace stitch pattern

Fair Isle - distinctive patterns in stranded color knitting, originally associated with the Scottish island, often used to describe many styles of multi-color knitting

faggot - lace stitch patterns using yarn-overs and decreases on every row

front (of work) - the side of work facing the knitter

garter stitch - basic stitch pattern; either knit every row or purl every row

gauge – (i) the number of stitches and rows to a given measurement, also known as tension (ii) a device for measuring the size of knitting needles

knitwise - inserting the needle as if to knit

manmade yarns - yarns from fibers made by chemical processes

multiple - a number of stitches grouped to form a repeat pattern along a row

natural fibers - animal hair, such as alpaca, mohair or wool; plant fiber, such as cotton or linen

panel - a group of stitches forming a self-contained pattern

purlwise - inserting needle into stitch as if to purl

repeat - a group of stitches or rows worked more than once to form a pattern

right side - the side of the stitch pattern viewed when the item is complete

shaping - using increases to make the fabric wider or decreases to make the fabric narrower, these can be placed at the edges, along a row, or for a dart

stockinette (as stocking stitch) basic stitch pattern, knit on right-side rows, purl on wrong-side rows

turning rows (short rows) - method of shaping by working part of a row, then turning the work

twisted stitches - single stitches worked through the back of the loop; not to be confused with twist stitch patterns

wrong side - the side of the stitch pattern that will not be seen when the item is complete

INDEX

2 and 3 Bobble Rib 96
3 Bobble Cable 98

A

abbreviations 26–7
Afterthought Flower 102
alpaca yarn 12
angora yarn 12
Argyll Checks 118
Armada Crosses 107

B

back of stitch, working into 44
balancing decreases 24, 39
balancing increases 23
Bamboo Rib 57
bands, knitted in 143
bar increase 23
beads 124, 132
Bell Pattern 103
Bellflower Blocks 77
Bellflower Motif 83
bias knitting 41
Birds Eye 88
Black, Sandy 151, 154
Blackberry Stitch 94, 96
Bliss, Debbie 153
blister 94
Bobble Blocks 97
Bobble and Braid Cable 97
Bobble and Wave 97
bobbles 89, 94–5, 95, 96, 97, 98, 99, 100, 101, 102
bouclé yarn 13
Branched Rib 77
Branching Leaves 83
Brioche Rib 55, 63
Brocade 73
Broken Blocks 46

Broken Double Rib 57
Broken Knit One, Purl One 56
Broken Moss Rib 61
Broken Stripes 116
Bugs 119
Butterfly Blocks 51
buttonholes 35, 143
buttons 35

C

cable cast-on 16
Cable Check 67
Cable Knot Rib 68
cable needle 10, 11, 64–5
cable stitches 10, 54, 64–72, 65, 97, 98, 100, 101, 103, 124
   in circular knitting 128
   with color knitting 144
   in entrelac 124, 127
Cabled Feather 86
Candlelight 90
Cartridge Belt Rib 60
cast-off seams 33
casting off 20–1, 33
casting on 16–17, 32–3
Celtic Vine 101
chain cast-off 20
Channel Island cast-on 32
charts 27
chenille yarn 13
chevron knitting 41
circular knitting 104, 124, 125, 128
   color 125, 128
   designing 145
circular needle 10, 36, 128
Close Stitch 59
Clustered Leaves 91
color knitting 32

with cables 144
circular 125, 128
intarsia 32, 114–23,
    115, 139, 104, 141
slip stitch 131
stranded 104–13, 105,
    125, 139, 140, 141
Cornish Lattice 47
cotton yarn 12, 54
crochet cast-off 21
crochet hook 11, 20, 21
cross stitch chart, adapting
    140
cross stitch embroidery 124
Crossed Rib 62

D
Daisy 53
Daisy border 132
Deckle Edge 69
decrease cast-off 21
decreasing 24, 38–9, 41
designing 136–7, 143,
    144, 145
    motifs 141
Diagonal K2, P2 Rib 58
Diamond edging 93
Diamond and Net 53
Diamond Spiral 90
Diamonds 123
double decrease 38–9, 41
double increase 40, 41
Double Moss Rib 62
Double Moss Stitch 47
Double Moss Stitch Heart
    50
Double Moss Stitch Star 50
double-pointed needles
    10, 128
double rib 54
dropped stitch, picking
    up 21

E
edging 93
Embossed Rib 61
embroidery 124, 133
entrelac 124, 125, 126–7

F
facings 32, 35
Fair Isle 104, 105
    flower borders 106
    peerie patters 106,
        109, 139
Falling Leaves 90
Fassett, Kaffe 148–9
fastenings 35
Feather and Fan 86
Feather Lace 91
Fern edging 93
Fisherman's Rib 55, 63
fixed needle 15
flecked yarn 12
Flower border 123
    Fair Isle 106
Flower Sprigs 100
Four-stranded Plait and
    Snake Cables 66
free needle 15
fully fashioned shaping 22

G
Garter Diamonds 48
garter stitch 18, 34
    in circular knitting
        128
    grafting 37
gauge 26, 28–9, 136,
    137, 138, 140
Gothic Lace 92
grafting 32, 36–7

H
Harding, Louisa 150
Harebells and Vine
    border 108
Hargreaves, Kim 151,
    152
Heart Leaf 101
Hearts and Chevrons
    52
hems 32, 34
Herringbone Twist 76
honeycomb pattern 65,
    67
Horseshoe Trellis 72

I
improvised yarn 13
in-the-round knitting
    see circular knitting
increasing 22, 23, 40, 41
intarsia knitting 32,
    114–23, 115, 139, 140,
    141
    designing 138
Inverted Pyramids 80

J
joining yarn 29

K
Knit One, Purl One Rib
    54, 56
knit and purl
    combinations 44–53
Knit Two, Purl Two Rib
    54, 57
knit stitch 18
knitting patterns: gallery
    146–7
    using 26–7
knotted cast-on 33

Knotted Rib 96
knots 94, 96, 103

L
lace edging 93
Lace Ladder 88
lace stitches 54, 84–93,
    85, 99
Large Leaf and Twists 99
Large Reindeer 111
Latvian Morning Stars 113
Latvian Stars 112
Leaf Cable 71
Leaf Cascade 92
leaves 94, 95, 99, 100, 101,
    102
Leaves 121
Leaves and Berries 89
left hand, using 14, 15
Leo 154
lifted-strand increase 23
Linen Stitch 51
linen yarn 12
linking in intarsia 114–15
Little Blocks 46
Little Cable Ribs 68
Little Slip Stitch
    Herringbone 51
Little Star with Shaded
    Waves 109
loop cast-on
loop knitting 124, 130

M
Macdonald, Julien 150
making up 30–1, 33, 36
marled yarn 12
Mawson, Katie 153
measurements 26, 136, 137
Mesh Lace edging 93
metallic yarn 13

Miniature Plait 76
mitered corners 34
mixed fiber yarn 12
Mock Cable 78
mohair yarn 12
Moss, Jean 150, 153
Moss Rib 61
Moss and Slip Stitch
    Rib 60
moss stitch 34, 44, 45,
    46, 128
motifs, designing 141, 143
    placing 142, 143

N
needles: holding 15
    size 28, 54
    types of 10

O
Oak Leaf 82
Old Shale 86
Ornate Cable with Leaf
    and Bobbles 100
Ovals and Flowers 73
Oxo and Honeycomb 67

P
Paired Leaves 91
Peruvian flower border 111
Peruvian hats 7, 155
Peruvian leaf border 112
picking up stitches 25
picot cast-off 33
Picot Heart 87
picot hem 34
Pierced Heart 87
Plait and Rib 69
Plaits and Ropes 66
pleats 124, 129
pressing 30, 31

CREDITS

Puff Stitch 102
purl stitch 19

R
rib 54–63, 55
    grafting 37
    sewing up 30
Ribbed Rope Cable 72
Robins, Freddie 154
rope pattern 64, 66, 72
Rosebuds and Ivy
    border 108
Roses and Vine border 108
roving yarn 12

S
Scandinavian Decorated
    Stripes 110
Scandinavian Heart 122
Scotch Faggot Cable 88
sequins 132
sewing up 30–1
Shadow Rib 59
shaping 22–5, 32, 37,
    38–9
silk yarn 12
Single Twisted Rib 56
slip stitch color knitting
    131
Slip-stitch Diagonals 81
Slip-stitch Lattice 79
Slip-stitch Ovals 81
slip stitch patterns 124
slipping stitches 44, 45
Small Hearts 87
Smocked Cable 70
Snowflake Border and
    Flea pattern 110
socks 125, 155
South American Bird 120
    geometric patterns
        109

hats 7, 155
    waves 112
Spots 117
Sprigs 117
Starflower with
    Diamond Flower
    Border 107
Starmore, Alice 152, 153
stockinette stitch 19, 27,
    137
    barred 45
    bias 41
    chevron 41
    circular knitting 128
    crossed 44
    embroidery on 124
    facings 35
    grafting 36
    hem 34
    intarsia 114
    reverse 19
    sewing up 30
    stranded color knitting
        104
Stocking Heel Rib 60
Storey, Martin 151
stranded color knitting
    104–13, 105, 125, 139,
    140, 141
Strawberry Bobble 99

T
tension 29
Textured Cable 71
thumb cast-on 17
Tilted Rib 58
Tiny Double Moss
    Diamonds 47
Tiny Trellis 76
Tree and Flags 52
Triple Nosegay 98
Triple Zigzag and Rope 69

tucks 124, 129
Tulip 89
Tulip Cable 72
Turkish Arrowhead 113
Turkish knitwear 155
Turkish sock pattern 113
turning rows 32, 33, 37
Twist Stitch Band 82
twist stitches 54, 74–83,
    75, 99
    circular knitting 128
Twisted Chevron 49
Twisted Diagonal 48
Twisted Little Check 48
Twisted Rib 79
Twisted Square Checker
    49
Two-texture Zigzag 70
Two-twist Lattice 78

W
Wave and Knots Cable
    103
wave pattern 64, 97, 103
Wave and Twist 77
weaving in yarn 104,105
Welted Rib 59
Welting 46
Westwood, Vivienne 151
Wide Rib 58
wool yarn 12, 54

Y
yarn: holding 14, 104
    types of 12–13

Z
zigzag pattern 65, 69,
    70, 74, 80
Zigzags 80
zippers 35

Quarto would like to thank and acknowledge the following for supplying pictures and items for photography reproduced in this book:

(Key: l left, r right, c center, t top, b bottom)

p5bl Debbie Bliss, tr Katie Mawson, br Jean Moss; p10-13 all items supplied by Coats Crafts UK *www.coatscrafts.co.uk*; p146bl&bc reproduced by kind permission from Coats Crafts UK (formerly Patons & Baldwins Ltd); p147br courtesy of Sirdar plc; p148-149 all designs by Kaffe Fassett, courtesy of Rowan/Photo: Joey Teller; p150tr&bc Jean Moss, cl Louisa Harding, courtesy of Rowan/Photo: Joey Teller, cr Julien MacDonald; p151tl Kim Hargreaves & cr Martin Storey, courtesy of Rowan/Photo: Joey Teller, tc Sandy Black/Photo: Paul Dennison, bl courtesy of Vivienne Westwood; p152cl&tc Alice Starmore from Aran Knitting, tr&bc Kim Hargreaveas, courtesy of Rowan/Photo: Joey Teller; p153l Jean Moss, tc Katie Mawson, bc Alice Starmore "Elephants" from the The Children' s Collection pub. Interweave Press 2000, r Debbie Bliss; p154l Freddie Robins, tc Sandy Black/Photo: Barbara Bellingham, br LEO; p155l Image Bank. The following items have been reproduced by kind permission of *Bella* magazine: grey ribbed cardigan on p.55, cables sweater on p.65; mouse on p.131.

All other photographs and illustrations are the copyright of Quarto Publishing plc.

While every effort has been made to credit contributors, Quarto would like to apologize should there have been any omissions or errors.